Towards a Typology of Intrametropolitan Manufacturing Location

A Case Study of the San Francisco Bay Area

University of Hull Publications

Occasional Papers in Geography No. 16
General Editor: H. R. Wilkinson
Professor of Geography in the
University of Hull

Towards a Typology of Intrametropolitan Manufacturing Location

A Case Study of the San Francisco Bay Area

Paul A. Groves

University of Hull Publications
1971

© The University of Hull 1971
SBN 90048091-2

Soc
HC
108
S7
G76

LIBRARY
FLORIDA STATE UNIVERSITY
TALLAHASSEE, FLORIDA

Made and Printed in England
by Hull Printers Limited
Great Gutter Lane, Willerby, Hull, HU10 6DH

CONTENTS

	Page
List of Figures	vi
List of Tables	viii
Acknowledgements	ix
INTRODUCTION	1
Chapter 1. THE THEORY OF INTRAMETROPOLITAN LOCATION OF MANUFACTURING	7
Chapter 2. THE EVOLUTION OF PRESENT MANUFACTURING LOCATIONAL PATTERNS IN THE BAY AREA	18
Chapter 3. A TYPOLOGY OF INTRAMETROPOLITAN MANUFACTURING LOCATION	42
Chapter 4. CONCLUSIONS	81
REFERENCES	86

FIGURES

		Page
1.	Orientation Map of the San Francisco Bay Area . .	3
2.	Manufacturing Employment—San Francisco Bay Area by Counties and Major Cities, 1860–1963 .	19
3.	San Francisco Bay Area—Manufacturing Employment, 1925.	21
4.	San Francisco Bay Area—Manufacturing Employment, 1963.	23
5.	Typical Manufacturing Flows for Local Market (A), Regional Market (B), and Multi-Regional Market (C) Industries	26
6.	Total Manufacturing Flows from Los Angeles, San Francisco, Pittsburgh, and Cincinnati based on 1963 Census of Transportation data . . .	28
7.	Location of Letterpress Printing Plants (S.I.C. 2751)— San Francisco Bay Area, 1963	31
8.	Location of Letterpress Printing (S.I.C. 2751), Lithographic Printing (S.I.C. 2752), and Newspaper (S.I.C. 2711) Plants in the Central Business District Area of San Francisco, 1963	34
9.	Location of Newspaper Plants (S.I.C. 2711)—San Francisco Bay Area, 1963	36
10.	Location of Metal Can Plants (S.I.C. 3411)—San Francisco Bay Area, 1963	45
11.	Location of Fabricated Structural Steel Plants (S.I.C. 3441)—San Francisco Bay Area, 1963 . . .	49
12.	Manufacturing Flows for the Paints and Varnishes (S.I.C. 2851) and Fabricated Structural Steel (S.I.C. 3441) Industries based on 1963 Census of Transportation data	51
13.	Location of Candy Plants (S.I.C. 2071)—San Francisco Bay Area, 1963	54

(Figures continued)

		Page
14.	Manufacturing Flows for the Motor Vehicles (S.I.C. 3711), Blast Furnaces and Steel Mills (S.I.C. 3312), and Malt Liquor (S.I.C. 2082) Industries based on 1963 Census of Transportation data	56
15.	Location of Malt Liquor Plants (S.I.C. 2082)—San Francisco Bay Area, 1963	58
16.	Location of Blast Furnaces and Steel Mills (S.I.C. 3312)—San Francisco Bay Area, 1963	60
17.	Manufacturing Flows for the Electric Measuring Instruments (S.I.C. 3611), Electronic Components, n.e.c. (S.I.C. 3679), and Semiconductors (S.I.C. 3674) Industries based on 1963 Census of Transportation data	63
18.	Location of Tungsten: Electronic Tubes Plants (S.I.C. 3673)—San Francisco Bay Area, 1963	65
19.	Location of Computing and Related Machine Plants (S.I.C. 3571)—San Francisco Bay Area, 1963	67
20.	Manufacturing Flows for the Canned Fruit and Vegetable (S.I.C. 2033) Industry based on 1963 Census of Transportation data	70
21.	Location of Canned Fruit and Vegetable Plants (S.I.C. 2033)—San Francisco Bay Area, 1963	72
22.	Location of Shipbuilding and Repairing Plants (S.I.C. 3731)—San Francisco Bay Area, 1963	75
23.	Location of Petroleum Refining Plants (S.I.C. 2911)—San Francisco Bay Area, 1963	77

TABLES

		Page
1.	Characteristics of Plants which will Abandon Central Sites (After Haig)	12
2.	Characteristics of Plants which will Cling to Central Sites (After Haig)	14
3.	San Francisco. Employment in Major Industries, 1880 .	24
4.	Major Industries of Santa Clara County, 1955–1963 .	38
5.	New Plants in the San Francisco Bay Area, 1958–1961 .	39
6.	San Francisco and Oakland Employment Fields, 1960 .	40
7.	Selected Industries of the San Francisco Bay Area, 1962	43
8.	Percentage of Shipments (Tons) by Selected Flow Distances for Los Angeles, San Francisco, Pittsburg, Cincinnati, and the United States, 1963 .	46
9.	Classification of Industries based on Site Requirements per Plant and per Production Employee. San Francisco Bay Area, 1963	47
10.	Typology of Intrametropolitan Manufacturing Locations	79

ACKNOWLEDGEMENTS

This paper was completed while the author was a Visiting Lecturer at the University of Hull during the academic year 1968–1969. The author is indebted to Professor H. R. Wilkinson for his help in the preparation of this paper, and also to Professors Allan Pred, James E. Vance, and Wallace Smith, all of the University of California at Berkeley, for their constructive criticism.

The maps were prepared by the cartographic staff of the Department of Geography, the University of Hull.

P.A.G.
College Park, Md.
May, 1970.

INTRODUCTION

The concentration of manufacturing within American metropolitan areas is an existing and continuous phenomenon. The antecedents of this concentration in a majority of the larger American metropolitan areas are to be found in the concomitant growth of industry and urbanization in the nineteenth century; this being part of a more generally recognized relationship existing in Western Europe and the United States in the period following the Industrial Revolution. The reasons for that growth have been the subject of critical evaluation (Lampard and Pred, 1966).

More than one-third of all manufacturing employees, as well as comparable amounts of production employees and value added by manufacturing, are currently found in the ten largest metropolitan areas of the United States. Despite this spatial concentration, relatively little analysis of the location of manufacturing within the urban area has been undertaken and this is in line with the comparative neglect of studies concerned with the location of specific activities within the city or metropolitan framework.

Generally, inquiries related to the city structure have taken two distinct directions. There are the theoretical explanations by Haig, Hoover and others that have been derived from the economists' notions about location theory (Isard, Thompson, Wendt, Alonso, 1964a), and there are theories (by Burgess, Hoyt, Ullman, Harris and others) which explore the location of activities within cities. The latter, of which manufacturing location is a part, remains the least developed. Jones comments as follows on the lack of theory on the location of activities within cities—'Important theoretical contributions to the description of components within the city have been seriously lacking in the period under consideration. Other aspects of urban theory have received massive contributions as has been shown' (Jones, p. 385).

The lack of more than a superficial and limited understanding of the distribution of manufacturing within the urban area, and the lack of economic theory concerned with those distribution patterns, leaves a broad gap in the existing body of urban studies. Partial responsibility for this lack of advance lies in the fact that the metropolitan area, and manufacturing within it, is the province of a large number of academic disciplines—economics, regional science, city planning, sociology, and geography—and, as a result, writings in the field are both dispersed and fragmentary. All of these fields are concerned with the metropolitan area, though the disposition to think of it as a meaningful unit of study is a comparatively recent phenomenon, dating largely from the work of Gras.

Such contributions as have been made to the understanding of the manufacturing function within urban areas are small in number; Haig, De Meirlier, Chinitz and Pred (1964a) are among those who have made significant contributions.

According to Gras, the metropolitan economy was a product of the continuation of technological and organizational changes associated with industrialization and the emergence of the metropolitan complex with the large city as a nucleus for an interdependent hinterland. The metropolitan area as a basically twentieth century phenomenon has, therefore, become a basic economic and social unit not only in regional and national economies but also in the world economy. The central city, the traditional unit of study, is only a nucleus or core within that larger functional area.

An understanding of the role of manufacturing within the urban area can only result from intensive research on a particular metropolitan area, at a high level of disaggregation with respect to industry groups, to enable some rational interpretation of location patterns. The distribution of manufacturing within the metropolitan area is remarkable for its diversity, as well as for its seemingly chaotic locational pattern of manufacturing. Beneath this superficial disorder and confusion, certain spatial regularities can be discerned if the structure of metropolitan manufacturing is viewed in terms of its evolution, the local friction of distance, and broad industrial categories which express similar locational tendencies.

Objective and Scope

The objective of study is twofold. First, to analyse the spatial distribution of manufacturing activity within the San Francisco Bay Area, with particular emphasis on the historical evolution of industry within the area, as a basic foundation for the understanding of existing patterns. Second, through the analysis of questionnaire data and mapped industrial patterns to formulate a typology of intrametropolitan industrial locations.

There are significant limitations on the scope of this study. The

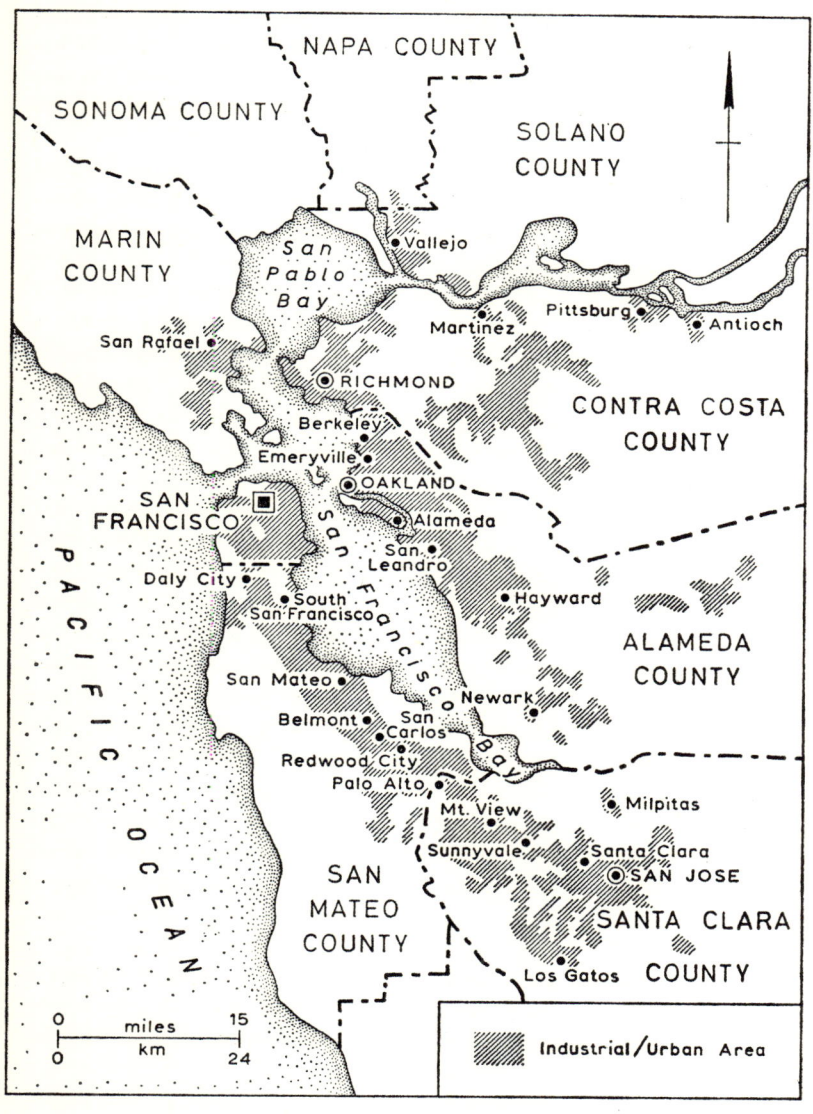

Fig. 1. Orientation Map of the San Francisco Bay Area.

analysis will focus on the San Francisco Bay Area, which is defined as the San Francisco-Oakland and San Jose Standard Metropolitan Statistical Areas. This is a seven county area, comprising Marin, Solano, Contra Costa, Alameda, Santa Clara, San Mateo, and San Francisco Counties (Figure 1). This can be considered as one economic unit, since manufacturing occurs in a single belt which overlaps the two Standard Metropolitan Statistical Areas, particularly on the west side of the Bay. In addition, the study focuses on the most important manufacturing industries of the Bay Area. The specific industry groups used for detailed study were those of the Standard Industrial Classification at the four-digit level*— a level of greater disaggregation than used in most previous studies.

Data Sources

Two basic types of data were required. First, those four-digit industries to be included in the study had to be identified. Only those industries that accounted for either one per cent of total Bay Area employment (2,293 employees), or one per cent of total Bay Area value added by manufacture ($27,021,000) in 1958 were considered for inclusion in the study (the list of industries selected for study would not have been materially changed by using the subsequent 1963 *Census of Manufactures* data). Excluded, though meeting the above requirements, were those industries not defined on a specific enough basis: for example, 'food industries, not elsewhere classified'.

The basic source of data for this information was the *1958 Census of Manufactures*. Using the data for the San Francisco-Oakland and San Jose Standard Metropolitan Statistical Areas, together with the 1958 Census, *Location of plants by Industry, County and Employment Size* and the 1958–59, *Large Manufacturers of the Bay Area* directory (where employment approximations had to be made because of disclosure problems), twenty-three separate four-digit industries were identified for inclusion in the study (Table 7).

Second, in view of the fact that the individual plant was to be the

---

*The Standard Industrial Classification operates in such a way that the industry definitions become progressively narrower with the addition of numerical digits. For the United States, there are 21 very broad 2-digit groups, 150 3-digit groups and 425 4-digit groups. The 4-digit level is the most detailed classification for which suitable spatial data for a study of this type is available.

Intrametropoltian Manufacturing Location

unit of study, all plants included in the selected industries had to be identified by street address and employment size. This was only possible because of the publication for 1962 of *The Bay Area Manufacturers Directory* by the San Francisco Bay Area Council; this was a unique publication—an equivalent was not published prior to 1962 and has not been published since. It was found, however, that this contained a number of errors and, therefore, was cross-checked against a variety of other sources. These other sources included *Polk Directories, Fortune Magazine Plant and Product Directory, Directory of Large Manufacturers (Bay Region Counties)*, and a variety of City and County manufacturing directories. The basic list obtained from the *1962 Bay Area Manufacturers Directory* was therefore checked as thoroughly as possible for incorrect locations, missing plants, and incorrect industry identification of individual plants. There is, as a result, a grand total of 981 plants comprising twenty-three separate industries included in the study.

Pertinent information was also obtained by means of a questionnaire. Some 653 questionnaires were distributed and 287 (approximately 44 per cent) usable returns were received.

Outline of Study

The study consists of four parts. First, a survey of the existing literature concerned with the intrametropolitan location of manufacturing. Second, a description of the historical evolution of manufacturing within the San Francisco Bay Area to 1963. Third, the formulation of a typology of intrametropolitan manufacturing locations based on detailed research of the San Francisco Bay Area, and fourth, a critical evaluation of the typology so produced.

CHAPTER I

THE THEORY OF INTRAMETROPOLITAN LOCATION OF MANUFACTURING

"At first glance, land utilization in an urban area such as New York and its environs appears to be without rhyme or reason, a confused and baffling welter of anomalies and paradoxes. The land is being used, most of it very intensively indeed . . . But the assignment of the land to the various uses seems to the superficial observer to have been made by the Mad Hatter at Alice's tea party . . . The confusion, of course, is more apparent than real. The deeper one delves into the reasons underlying the present layout, the more distrustful he becomes of sweeping indictments of its soundness and efficiency. Most of the apparent anomalies and paradoxes dissolve into common-places when subjected to serious study." (Haig, p. 31).

IN this manner, Haig outlined both the problem and the solution involved in the analysis of intrametropolitan manufacturing location. His detailed analysis of the New York area in 1962 resulted in a theoretical approach to land use in the urban area which stressed the two components of rent and transportation costs. Weber had earlier laid emphasis on transportation costs in his theory of general industrial location, but added to this factor, as deviating influences, both labour cost and agglomeration advantages. Though his theory is not concerned *per se* with metropolitan location, he does state that for 'local orientation (of industry) within the railway station unit, with its street net system, exactly the same rules of orientation will be operative in detail which determine the orientation at large for the whole country.' (Weber, p. 87).

Transportation

The structural role given to transportation has been central to the field of urban land economics for half a century. Hurd in 1903 'succinctly formulated the interrelationship of urban land values and the urban transportation system, a proposition scarcely modified in current writing on the problem.' (Wingo, p. 24). It remained for Haig to spell out Hurd's formulation in greater detail. Haig argued that the centre of the city represented the market point, and that separation from that point involved transportation costs. 'Since there is insufficient space at the centre to accommodate all the activities which could derive advantages from location there, the most central sites are assigned to those activities which can best utilize the advantages, while the others take the less accessible locations.' (Haig, p. 39). In this manner an order of precedence of activities is worked out through competitive bidding. Haig and subsequent contributors recognized that a basic ordered system of land uses resulted from the operation of economic forces in society. Ratcliff, for example, pointed out that 'the locational pattern of urban areas is a reflection of basic economic forces and that this arrangement of people, buildings and activities in urban concentrations at strategic points on the web of transportation lines is part of the economic mechanism of society.' (Ratcliff, 1949, p. 368).

The Hurd-Haig analytical framework and conclusions have been accepted by virtually all land economists, and only recently have come under critical appraisal. Wendt, for example, has suggested various other factors that affect the competitive bidding for land.

The point of maximum accessibility having the highest land values, the 'One hundred per cent location', is the central point around which urban land use patterns are formulated. In its simple form there is one such focal point, in its more sophisticated form the theory evolves around a number of focal points. Mayer provides evidence of the peaking of land values at major traffic intersections, differential peakings according to relative importance of the intersections, and the association of such peaked land values with use of the land at and around the intersections. Since such focii 'provide one observable set of central locations ... they can provide clues to the eventual understanding of the larger problem of competitive bidding for urban land and resulting patterns of land use.' (Garrison, p. 61).

In terms of relevance to intrametropolitan manufacturing location Pred has the most concise criticisms to offer on the theories of the maximum accessibility or central location advocates. He argues that such theories do not take into account that 'markets served by some metropolitan manufacturers are discontinuous, non-local and distant; that transport costs are immaterial to site selection decisions in many industries; and that no account is taken of the desirability or undesirability of core locations for specific kinds of industries' (Pred 1964a, p. 171).

Descriptive Schemes

The emphasis on location as the basis for urban land values is derived from von Thünen in the agricultural case, and from Hurd-Haig in the urban land use case. The simplest model that illustrates this notion is the 'concentric circle' scheme, one of four identifiable idealized descriptive schemes with relevance to the intrametropolitan location of manufacturing. The concentric circle theory of urban growth developed by Burgess goes no further than delimiting a zone of warehousing and light manufacturing adjacent to the central business district. The 'sector' theory, anticipated by Hurd, but developed by Hoyt from data collected for about two hundred cities, describes a city in terms of a series of sectors or wedges extending outward from the core. Each wedge is characterized by one type of land use. In terms of industrial land use the greatest relevance of this theory relates to growth along transportation lines radiating from the city centre (Pegrum).

Interestingly enough, Hurd observed that city growth was due to aggregation at the edges and pressure from the centre. 'Central growth takes place both from the heart of the city and from each subcentre of attraction, and axial growth pushes into outlying territory by means of railroads, turn-pikes and street railroads.' (Hurd, p. 15). In some ways this represents a simultaneous realization of concentric growth, sector growth, and of the importance of a number of nuclei in metropolitan land-use pattern development.

The third descriptive scheme is that of Harris and Ullman. This describes the city as a series of nuclei, each characterized by an activity or group of related activities requiring specialized facilities best provided by the sites and locations that it occupies. This theory provides for a wholesaling light manufacturing nucleus, a heavy manufacturing nucleus and an industrial suburb. Writing in 1962, Ullman stated that 'the metropolis of today and increasingly in the future is not only one city, but a federation of general and special centres. As such (the city) is likely to have several hearts better located than one, and basically will be better off because of reduction in travel time, congestion, and utilization of better sites;' this, he suggests, strengthens the multiple nuclei concept suggested in the earlier 'Nature of Cities.' (Ullman, 1962, p. 22).

The fourth descriptive scheme is that of Isard. Isard modifies Löschian hexagonal market areas in terms of the gradation in densities that would be expected from the concentration of centres given in the Lösch system. Lösch insisted upon using an assumption of uniform density throughout his economic landscape in spite of the fact that his centres were of different sizes. Isard modifies the market areas so that they grade in size from small around a centre to large away from that centre. The urban land use pattern Isard produces contains four separate industrial districts. Concentrated in each of the industrial districts are all producers of any given commodity. Isard admits, that this land use pattern 'represents one of the many possible brews of (1) intuition, (2) logic and analytic principles relating to the interaction of general forces governing land use, and (3) facts. It is not a rigorous theoretical definition.' (Isard, p. 280). Criticism of Isard's scheme is based on the fact that there is no manufacturing district immediately adjacent to the central business district and that the industries represented are either concentrated in a single district or ubiquitous—and that no patterns intermediate to these extremes are suggested.

Two general criticisms can be made of all the above theories, both theoretical and schematic. First, manufacturing is just one activity being treated in the total realm of urban economic activity. Second, when the first criticism is not applicable as with Weber and Isard, then manufacturing is not viewed in a sufficiently disaggregated form to enable any meaningful analysis to be made. Too often, the only disaggregation is into light or heavy industry, or intensive versus extensive industry, with little effort made to meaningfully distinguish between them (Smith, W., Florence, Kenyon).

Empirical Studies

Of the empirical studies of some relevance to intrametropolitan manufacturing location, many contribute very little to the body of knowledge necessary for the formulation of a significant theory. Some have been included because they illustrate a particular approach. It is considered that the ideal study of intrametropolitan manufacturing location should give due recognition to four basic elements, First, that the study apply to a total metropolitan area, not to just one segment of that metropolis. Second, that manufacturing be treated in a highly disaggregated manner, (Standard Industrial Classification 4-digit level), so that meaningful groupings of locationally similar industries can be established. Third, that there be cartographic representation of the location of industries. Fourth, that from the empirical data collected and analysed there be some attempt at the formulation of a typology of intrametropolitan manufacturing location. Such a typology should take cognizance of factors such as central versus non-central locations, market areas, transportation costs, and linkage to wholesale, retail and other manufacturing functions. As Jones has pointed out in a rather broader context 'Further development in the whole body of urban economic theory must await major advances in the theory of intraurban distribution.' (Jones, p. 657).

Empirical works of the last fifty years cover a broad spectrum from the marginally relevant to the core works in the field. The latter grouping is composed of only four studies which fulfil the requirements outlined above to a major degree. At the other end of the spectrum are the land use studies (Harvey, Loewenstein, 1965, Bartholomew) and the purely descriptive studies (Thomas, Smith, W., Griffin, Kerr, Gonen) both at a level high of generalization, and neither of which extends far beyond providing a broad picture of urban land uses. They fail to add to a real understanding of intrametropolitan manufacturing location because they are couched in terms of aggregated land use types rather than the individual manufacturing plant, and fail significantly to provide cartographic representation except at a highly generalized level. Another approach is that exemplified by Estall and Martin who studied Greater London by examining the ten districts that compose that area; the difficulty here is that these districts are imposed administrative units which are not meaningful units of analysis. In a more recent study on the industrial geography of the London region Martin has collected and mapped data for a number of relatively disaggregated industries within a kilometric grid square framework (Martin, 1966). Though the study provides an excellent descriptive, if somewhat aggregated, account of the location of industry in London, there is no attempt at the production of a theory of intraurban industrial location.

TABLE 1

CHARACTERISTICS OF PLANTS WHICH WILL
ABANDON CENTRAL SITES

List of Characteristics:
1. Comparatively large size;
2. Time or service factor unimportant;
3. Large ground area per person required;
4. Nuisance features (odors, noise, high fire hazard, etc.);
5. Specialized buildings required;
6. Serious problem of waste disposal; and
7. Large quantities of fuel and/or water required.

Examples	Characteristics as listed above						
Heavy chemicals	1	2	3	4	5	6	7
Copper smelting and refining	1	2	3	4	5	6	7
Sugar refining	1	2	3	4	5	....	7
Iron foundries	1	2	3	4	5	6	....
Explosives	1	2	3	4	5	....	....
Paint, soap, and fertilizer	1	2	3	4	5	....	....
Slaughtering	1	....	3	4	5	6	....
Textile finishing	1	....	3	4	....	....	7
Petroleum refining	1	....	3	4	5	....	....
Lumber and planing mills	1	....	3	....	5	....	....
Candy (large, machine type)	1	2	3	....	....	....	....
Technical instruments (non-local type)	1	2	....	....	5	....	....
Periodical printing	1	2	....	....	....	....	....
Book printing	1	2	....	....	....	....	....
Bookbinding	1	2	....	....	....	....	....
Job printing (large runs)	1	2	....	....	....	....	....
Jewelry (medium-priced)	1	2	....	....	....	....	....
Women's underwear, kimonos, corsets, etc.	1	2	....	....	....	....	....

Another group of studies that can be identified are those in which the decentralization or diffusion of manufacturing in the metropolitan area is the major theme. These are important in that they give clues to the changing needs of the manufacturing plant over time (Mitchell, Linge, Logan, 1964a and b). The majority of them treat manufacturing in an aggregated form which does not allow for a rigorous theoretical formulation from the data. One of the more detailed studies in this group is that of Philadelphia which shows considerable detail in the cartographic representation of industrial movement on a S.I.C. 2-digit level (Alderson Associates).

Recognition should also be made of the recent work of Stevens, Brackett and Coughlin, which contains a listing of major locational characteristics for each 4-digit S.I.C. manufacturing industry, but which is of limited value because of its lack of spatial consideration.

Studies in which the individual plant is the unit of analysis, in which considerable data is mapped, but which provide no theoretical formulation are common. These may be from an historical standpoint (Hall), from a rather specialized standpoint (Rodgers), or an analysis of a static pattern (Stefaniak, 1962, Janasson). They again suffer from insufficient disaggregation of the manufacturing element.

The four studies which are considered to be of particular relevance to this study are those of Haig, De Meirlier, Chinitz, and Pred. These are of special importance in that they represent the only attempts to derive theoretical constructs from empirical data. This is not to decry the studies mentioned above for generally they were not directed at the production of theory but considered the description or analysis of a particular function, development process or area as an end in itself.

Haig's urban land theory has already been discussed. It is important to acknowledge that his theory was based upon extensive empirical data, namely the twelve special studies carried out in connection with the *Regional Survey of New York and its Environs*. The data collected in these special studies covered nine broad industry groups which in turn were disaggregated into a total of thirty-one sub-divisions. For each of these sub-divisions, maps were prepared showing the distribution of each industry for the years 1900 and 1922. Monographs on each of the nine major industrial groups were prepared in which the shifts in the location of industrial plants in the twenty year period were discussed and the reasons for that shift analysed. Haig attached particular importance to functional differentiation in his 1927 monograph. He considered it essential to differentiate between fabrication, selling, and storage functions and placed emphasis on the relative cohesion of functions between different industries. 'The extent to which a business may with profit separate physically certain of its functions from the others varies greatly. In some cases the packet of functions is loosely tied, in others it is tied tightly.' (Haig, p. 37). As a result, Haig's definition of manufacturing is strict; that is, it is synonymous with fabrication.

Haig notes that there are certain industries which, in the absence of special measures such as zoning, will adhere to sites in the centre of the metropolis. He presents the characteristics of those industries (Table 1) that may be expected to abandon central sites if they have not already done so. He then outlines (Table 2) those 'symptoms by which the type of plant which clings to the central locations may be easily recognised'. (Haig, p. 104). Haig then proceeds to point out

TABLE 2

CHARACTERISTICS OF PLANTS WHICH WILL
CLING TO CENTRAL SITES

List of Characteristics:
1. No specialized buildings required;
2. Time or service factor an important element;
3. Specialized, unstandardized, highly skilled work;
4. Low ground area per worker required;
5. Comparatively small scale;
6. Obsolete buildings suitable;
7. Close contact with market required;
8. Highly seasonal, fluctuating labor force; and
9. Style factor important.

Examples	Characteristics as listed above								
Women's cloaks and dresses	1	2	3	4	5	6	7	8	9
Men's clothing	1	2	3	4	5	6	7	8	9
Knitted outerwear	1	2	3	4	5	6	7	8	9
Textile small wares	1	2	3	4	5	6	7	8	9
High-grade jewelry	1	2	3	4	5	....	7	....	9
Small job printing	1	2	3	....	5	6	7	8	....
Special furniture and cabinet work	1	2	3	....	5	....	7	....	9
Metal assembling and service plants	1	2	3	4	5	6	....	....	....
Technical instruments (local type)	1	2	3	....	5	6	....	....	....
Cigars (high-grade, hand-made product)	1	....	3	4	5	6	....	....	....
Photo-engraving	1	2	3	4	....	6	....	....	....
Cosmetics and toilet preparations	1	....	....	4	....	6	....	....	....
Metropolitan newspapers	....	2	....	....	....	....	7	....	....
Biscuits and crackers	....	....	....	4	....	....	....	8	....
Candy (large, hand-work type)	....	....	....	4	....	....	....	8	....

way certain industries may be expected to move east or west from central New York: the attraction of areas where there is excess female labour, such as the Pennsylvania coalfields; the tenacious clinging of some industries to waterfront locations; the highly perishable nature of the products of some industries; the great increases in bulk or weight in the final stages of some industrial production and, as a result, location primarily with reference to local distribution factors; and, the growth of local industries to serve an increasing population (Haig, pp. 104–6). These factors are, of course, highly relevant to metropolitan industrial analysis.

One further point concerning Haig's work should be made. He was analysing the major economic activities of the New York area in order to facilitate planning for that area. In that respect, Haig considered the task of the planner to be 'largely that of reducing the friction of space. Transportation, to, from and within the city is, consequently of fundamental importance. It is necessary to proceed on assumptions as to where things belong according to economic criteria.' (Haig, p. 9). There is little doubt that the study of Haig and his associates provided a vast quantity of empirical data, interesting mapped industrial location material, and a body of theory which Ratcliff has called 'the very cornerstone of modern land economics.' (Ratcliff, 1955, p. 126).

The contribution of De Meirleir (pp. 115–133) was the recognition that a classification of manufacturing industries in an urban area could be made on the basis of the market for the industry's products together with the origin of the basic raw materials used in the industry. On this basis, a fourfold classification of industries in the West Central Area of Chicago was proposed. These were (1) local market industries with locally obtained basic raw materials, (2) local market industries with nationally (not locally) obtained basic raw materials, (3) national market industries with locally obtained raw materials, and (4) national market industries with nationally obtained basic raw materials. The analysis was not extended, however, and a detailed analysis of individual industries was not undertaken to support the basis for the classification.

Chinitz's study, produced thirty-three years after that of Haig, is the third core contribution to the theory of intrametropolitan manufacturing location. He states that the New York Region as a location for manufacturing 'is much more attractive to some industries than it is to others. Our object is to understand how developments in freight transport have changed these varying degrees of attraction in the past and are likely to change them in the future.' (p. 91). In his analysis Chinitz is concerned with three broad groups of industries which account for 80 per cent of the New York Region's manufacturing employment.

The first group consists of industries—mainly in the clothing (apparel) and printing categories—which are highly concentrated in the region, and whose locational pattern is heavily influenced by the need for fast communication with suppliers, subcontractors, and customers. These are the 'communication-oriented' industries. The second group consists of local-market industries, such as newspapers and bakeries. Specifically, they are defined as those industries which ship more than half their tonnage to markets inside the Region. The third group consists of national-market industries which ship more than half their tonnage to markets outside the Region. Significant differences are noted in this latter group based on size of plant and value of product.

Each of these industrial groupings is then analysed. 'Communication-oriented industries are found to be heavily concentrated in New York City, which accounts for about four-fifths of the New York Region's employment in this group. National-market industries are analysed in terms of the size of the plant and value of the products. Chinitz, however, pays some homage to the concentric ring school of analysis by dividing the Region into three areas. These are New York City, the Inner Belt, and the Outer Belt. This unfortunately is the extent of his spatial analysis for there is no cartographic representation either. Chinitz, therefore, produces a sound typology based to a large degree on an extensive transportation survey of the manufacturing plants of the Region, but his study fails in the number of ways. These failures are primarily related to his failure to carry his analysis further with respect to mapped disaggregated manufacturing industries.

The most detailed sub-division of metropolitan manufacturing industry produced to date is that of Pred. He groups industry into 'seven flexible types, each of which, theoretically, should be characterized by distributional patterns with a unique set of attributes, including, in some instances, randomness' (Pred, 1964a, p. 174). Each of the seven types illustrated by examples drawn from the San

Intrametropolitan Manufacturing Location

Francisco Bay Area. The typology is based on a number of factors; raw material origins, markets, external economies, value of product, and transportation considerations both as regards media and transport rates (pp. 174–80).

The Pred typology is as follows:
(1) Ubiquitous Industries Concentrated near the Central Business District (including local market, non-local raw materials);
(2) Local Market Industries with Local Raw Material Sources;
(3) Centrally Located 'Communication-Economy' Industries;
(4) Non-Centrally Located 'Communication-Economy' Industries;
(5) Non-Local Market Industries with High Value Products;
(6) Non-Local Market Industries on the Waterfront;
(7) Industries Oriented Towards National Markets.

This typology is the most systematic of those outlined in this short and somewhat incomplete, review of existing relevant literature. It should be noted, however, that this (along with other typologies discussed) does not meet the basic criteria for an empirical study set forth earlier in this chapter. Pred's typology, for example, is not based on the analysis of a given set of data, but rather represents generalizations concerning 'the logical patterning of locational trends.' Emphasis is placed in this study on the fact that a range of industries, selected solely on the criterion of importance to the industrial structure of the San Francisco Bay Area, was studied and that the typology was produced from an analysis of that *given* group of industries.

CHAPTER II

THE EVOLUTION OF PRESENT MANUFACTURING LOCATIONAL PATTERNS IN THE BAY AREA

In 1963 San Francisco was the largest single manufacturing city in the Bay area; although it accounted for only 21 per cent of manufacturing employment, compared with 75 per cent at the turn of the century. A marked decentralization of manufacturing activity during the twentieth century is apparent, caused primarily by the development of new modes of transportation. In the period when rail and waterways were the most efficient means of moving goods from one place to another, manufacturing activity clustered in the large cities which were at the nodal points of these transport systems. As late as 1920, Oakland and San Francisco were the dominant manufacturing cities in the Bay Area based on their deepwater ports and railroad facilities.

With the advent of the automobile and truck, and with a highway system increasing in efficiency and mileage, manufacturers were freed from their dependence upon fixed lines of communication. As a result, they were able to consider other factors in choosing their locations, and this led to an increasing trend to location outside of the older urban core areas.

By mid-century, however, the decentralizing effect of the truck and the automobile had been largely spent, and a variety of forces favouring new metropolitan concentration came to the fore. In the Bay Area, today, the electronics industry is highly concentrated around Palo Alto; a function of the need to keep abreast of the latest innovations and forthcoming contracts. Jet transport and the increasing importance of piggy-back transport have also acted as breaks on decentralization, for the expense of constructing a modern new jet airport or of maintaining the complex and expensive terminal facilities required for efficient piggy-back operation can only be supported by concentrations of people and large concentrated markets.

The history of manufacturing growth in the San Francisco Bay Area is largely that of the growth of subsidiary centres of industrial

Intrametropolitan Manufacturing Location

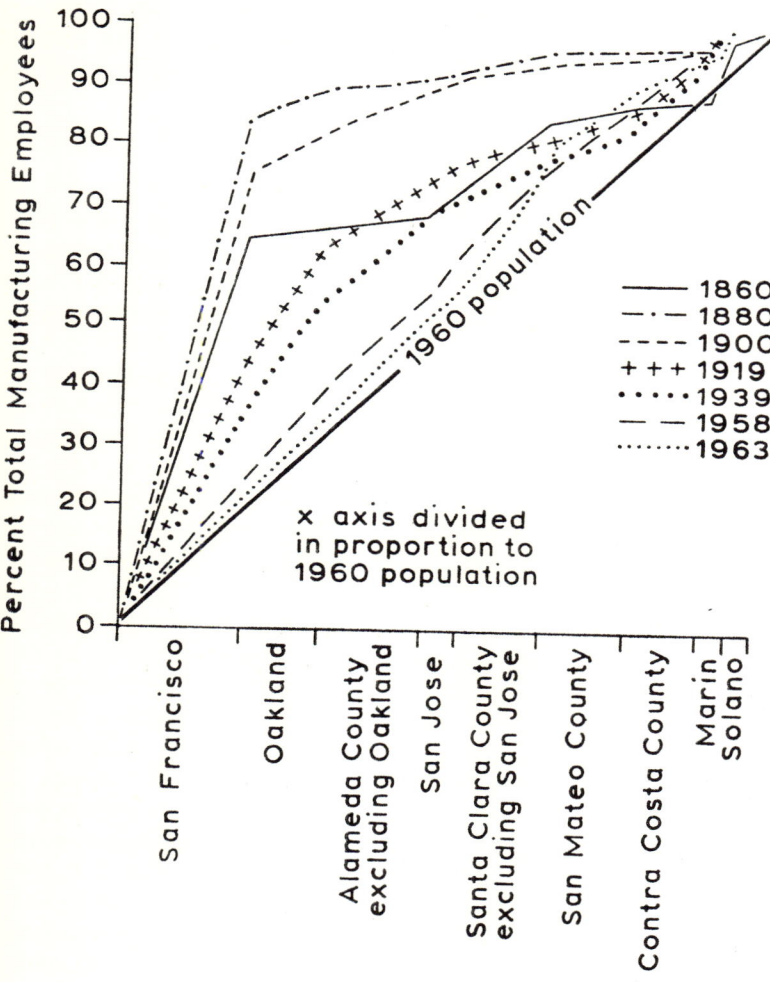

FIG. 2. MANUFACTURING EMPLOYMENT—SAN FRANCISCO BAY AREA BY COUNTIES AND MAJOR CITIES, 1860-1963.

concentration at the expense of the dominance of the original 'core' cities of San Francisco and Oakland (Figure 2). An understanding of this growth is a necessary prelude to any analysis of manufacturing in the area.

Industrial Growth Prior to 1906

The growth of manufacturing in the Bay Area before the First World War was limited. It was characterized largely by small factories serving the local and northern California market, and displayed a high degree of concentration in the city of San Francisco. Because of its strategic location in relation to the gold fields, San Francisco was the port of entry for thousands of immigrants to California, and became the supply base for the mining operations. The period of the gold rush marked the first appreciable movement of population into California, and its dramatic effect can be illustrated by the rapid growth of San Francisco. In mid-1848 San Francisco had about 500 residents; by 1850, close to 35,000. This rapid increase in population resulted in a demand for all kinds of manufactured goods that could not be met by local industry. Together with the problems caused by the slow, uncertain, and costly trip round Cape Horn or over the Isthmus of Panama, this demand presented the opportunity 'to establish profitable industry in the face of high labour cost and crude equipment.' (Niklason, p.397).

Food products were in great demand, and, as rapidly as the development of agriculture warranted it, flour mills, canneries, and lumber mills were established as well as factories for the production of farm equipment. Such industry was established throughout the Bay Area; fruit canneries in the Santa Clara Valley; flour mills in Oakland, San Francisco and Vallejo; tanneries in Redwood City and Benicia based on local slaughterhouse activities, and farm equipment in San Jose and Benicia. As a result of the broad distribution of the raw materials utilized in the agriculturally based industry, Bay Area manufacturing in 1860 was dispersed to a degree which was not duplicated until the 1920's.

Even more important, especially in its relationship to the development and concentration of manufacturing in San Francisco, was the demand for mining equipment and supplies and for transportation equipment. Wagon making and shipbuilding developed

Intrametropolitan Manufacturing Location

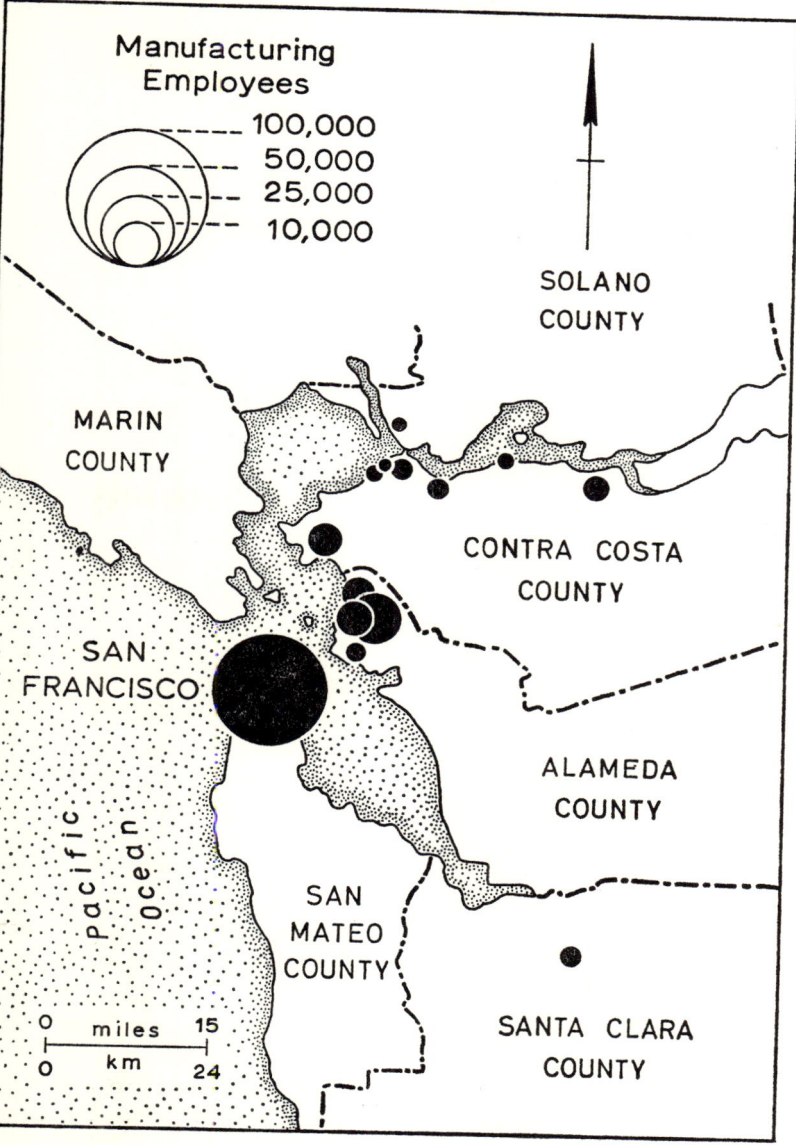

Fig. 3. San Francisco Bay Area—Manufacturing Employment, 1925.

along with the manufacturing of mining and agricultural implements. These, in turn, gave rise to a variety of related enterprises, particularly foundries and machine shops. The large number of repairs required was sufficient to give a foothold to a number of industries.

As local wheat had encouraged the grinding of flour, impracticability of movement over long distances encouraged breweries, local fruit and vegetables encouraged canneries, and mining promoted foundry activities.

In the 1860's high wages were the general rule, but the concentration of Chinese labour in San Francisco provided cheap labour for the limited number of industries in which they were allowed to seek employment. 'Without them a number of industries like the making of shoes, underclothing and cigars could not have been maintained.' (Bancroft, p. 69). To these industries might also be added woolen mill products. The Chinese were the target for strong discriminatory practices in the last part of the nineteenth century; they were paid lower wages than the whites, confined to certain industries, and were finally subjected to legal exclusion from California under a series of Exclusion Acts from 1882 to 1902. As a result, in many industries the wage rates were high, and, after the completion of the transcontinental railroad link, industry was subjected to competition from the Eastern states. The rapid growth of the railroads in this period resulted in decreasing transportation costs from the East.* Consequently, Eastern manufacturers-particularly in those fabricated products having potential thresholds in the Bay Area, were able to absorb transport costs from the East and sell in the Bay Area at prices the local manufacturers could not meet.

The transcontinental railway also boosted certain Bay Area industries, particularly fruit canning and fruit drying. In 1872, 182,090 pounds of canned fruits were shipped to Eastern points; by 1888 when the freight rate on canned fruit had dropped from an earlier $3·51 per 100 pounds to $0·94, shipments had reached 39,281,340 pounds (Bancroft, p. 743).

With the growth of local railroads, the wheat ports of Port Costa, Vallejo and Martinez benefited from their ability to draw from a

---

*Railroad mileage in the United States doubled between 1865 and 1873, and doubled again from 1873 to 1887.

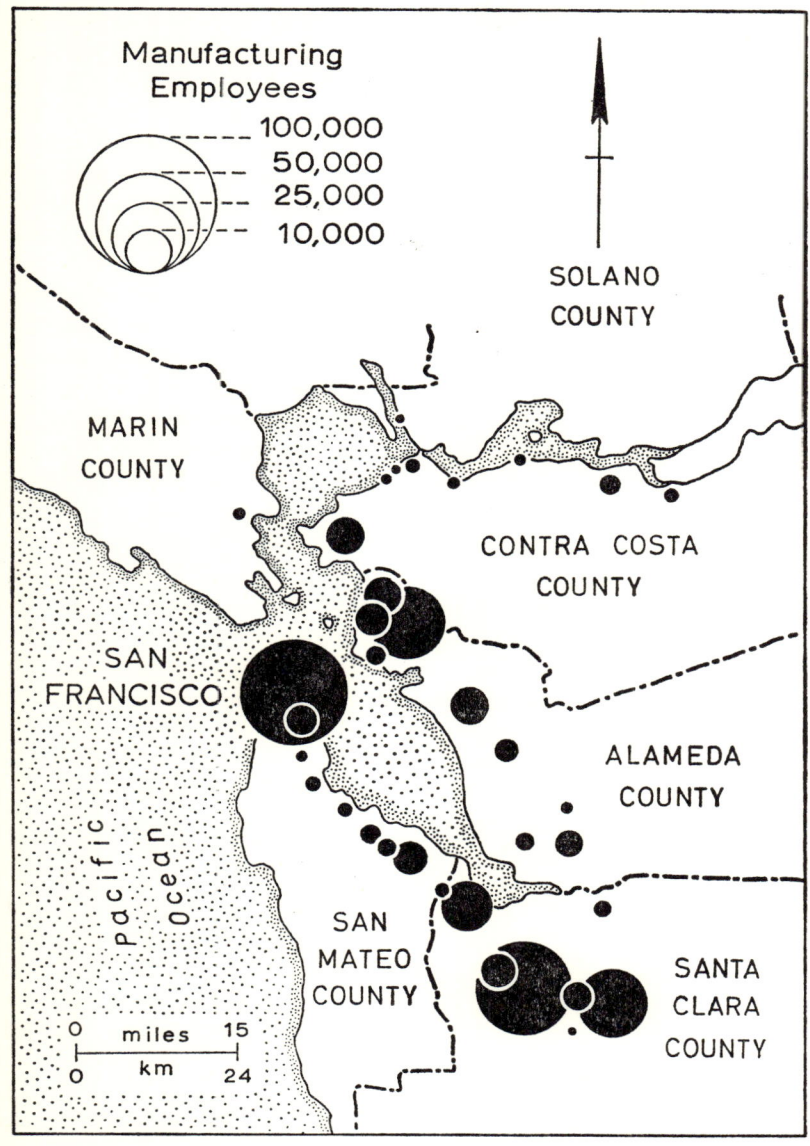

Fig. 4. San Francisco Bay Area—Manufacturing Employment, 1963.

wider hinterland. The Bay Area, as a whole, benefited from the ballast cargoes carried from Europe by the wheat carrying ships. In this way high grade coal was brought from Europe to the Bay Area often at little or no cost. Pig iron and scrap iron was also a ballast cargo, and much of this found its way to Oakland, where a small scale iron and steel industry developed. The Judson Manufacturing Company of Emeryville, established on a nine acre site in 1885, was the largest iron and steel company to result from this return cargo.

Largely as a result of its position as the western terminal for the trans-continental railroad, Oakland had by 1880 acquired a small industrial base. San Francisco still acted as the port and major manufacturing centre for the Bay Area, but Oakland had assumed the role of railroad terminus. The leading industries in Oakland in 1880 were shipbuilding, lumber planing, malt liquors, flour and grist mill products, and metal working. In comparison with San Francisco, however, its manufacturing employment was insignificant; 1,387 manufacturing employees as against 28,442 in San Francisco. (Table 3).

By 1880, close to 89 per cent of manufacturing employment in the Bay Area was accounted for by San Francisco and Oakland (Figure 2). This was the high point of concentration; for the next 80 years decentralization of manufacturing was to characterize the Bay Area.

By 1890, Alameda, Berkeley and San Jose shared dominion with San Francisco and Oakland in residential development. though at that time these centres had little in the way of industry. A

TABLE 3

SAN FRANCISCO. EMPLOYMENT IN MAJOR INDUSTRIES, 1880.

Tobacco, cigars and cigarettes*	3,428 employees
Boots and shoes*	3,344 ,,
Foundry and machine shops	1,921 ,,
Clothing mens*	1,915 ,,
Printing and publishing	1,527 ,,
Carpentering	1,192 ,,
Malt liquors	813 ,,
Canned and preserved fruits and vegetables	646 ,,

(Asterisks—industries in which Chinese labour was dominant)

Source: *1880 Census of Manufactures*

Intrametropolitan Manufacturing Location

possible exception was San Jose, which was a canning and dried fruit centre. Each of these cities was tributary to San Francisco, and each was connected with that city by some developed transportation media. Oakland, Berkeley, and Alameda were linked to each other by street-running railroad lines, and to San Francisco by ferry. As early as 1873 there were some 2·7 million ferry passengers between Oakland and San Francisco, and within four years this figure had doubled. This reflects strongly the dormitory function of the East Bay cities. San Jose had been linked by railroad to San Francisco since 1864; and San Mateo, Burlingame, San Carlos and Belmont developed as a result of this link. All this emphasizes the leading role played by San Francisco, a role reflected in its dominant position in the industrial, commercial and population patterns of the Bay Area in the closing decade of the nineteenth century.

From 1870 to the time of the earthquake and fire, San Francisco contained more than 50 per cent of Bay Area population. The earlier years of this period were marked by a decline in gold rush 'fever' and many miners retraced their footsteps of earlier years and returned to San Francisco. To the miners were added Chinese labourers whose work on the transcontinental railroad was finished. Thus the population was increasing quite rapidly, though skilled labour was at a premium, and wage rates, except in those industries employing Chinese, were high. To these problems was added that of a scarcity of certain raw materials.

The fuel handicap was particularly severe. The Mount Diablo coal mines which operated from 1860 to 1902 were never a satisfactory local source of fuel for the Bay Area. During the late nineteenth century, imports of European coal at California ports amounted to 75 per cent of the coal tonnage imported into the United States (*Mining and Scientific Press*). 'The fuel handicap continued until an adequate and sustained output of petroleum was assured about 1910.' (Niklason, p. 398). By 1910, also, hydroelectric power generated in the Sierra Nevada Mountains was being transmitted to the North Bay, Oakland and San Francisco. These two relatively inexpensive sources of energy provided an important stimulant to Bay Area industry, which had been hindered by inadequate and expensive fuel supplies.

The first of the oil refineries which today give the North Bay industrial lanscape much of its character was erected in 1896 by

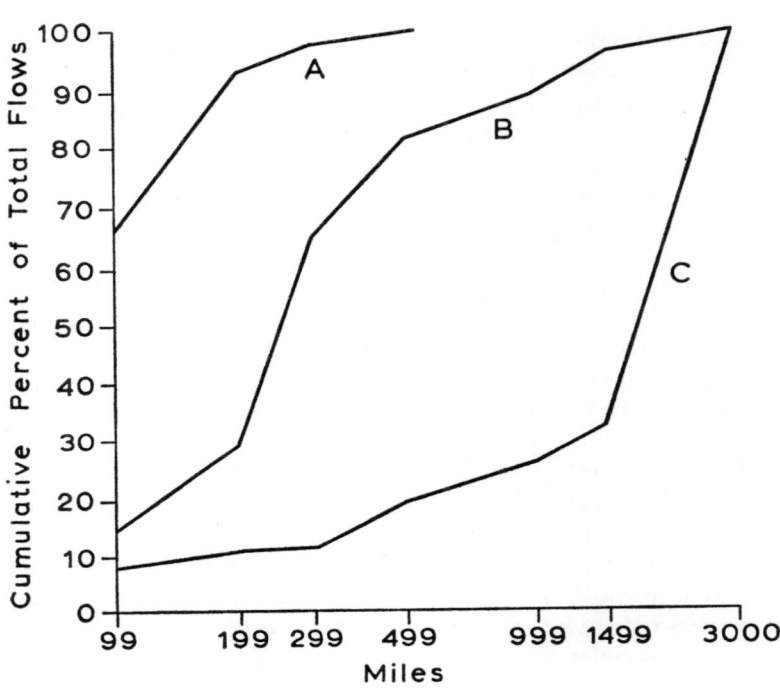

Fig. 5. Typical Manufacturing Flows for Local Market (A), Regional Market (B), and Multi-Regional Market (C) Industries

the Union Oil Company at Oleum. Not long thereafter Standard Oil of California (1901), Tidewater (1911) and Shell (1913) began operation. The Union refinery received its crude oil from Southern California by ship, the Tidewater and Shell refineries received most of their crude oil from pipelines from the San Joaquin Valley oil fields.

> 'The northern coast of Contra Costa County was the first location where crude oil pipelines from the San Joaquin Valley met deep water. This location not only gave the refineries direct access to the centre of the California market, but also access to the terminal facilities of rail and shipping lines where were both distributors and users of petroleum products.' (Marr, p.II-6).

Other industries dependent on deep water facilities developed in the same period. The California and Hawaii Sugar Refining

Corporation established a sugar cane refinery at Crockett in 1906, and Columbia Steel's Pittsburg plant was erected in 1910. By 1910, therefore, the Bay Area had an assured supply of energy and was producing steel locally for the first time at Pittsburgh and South San Francisco. Starting from a small base of industry located largely in San Francisco and importing iron and steel as considerable quantities of coal, the Bay Area had evolved to a position where diversified manufacturing, rather than fabricating specialized products for the local extractive and agricultural industries, was more characteristic.

Along with new industries seeking locations outside San Francisco because of space requirements, a number of other industries were moving from the city itself. Both the smelting and explosives industries moved from San Francisco to Contra Costa County between 1879 and 1884. The extensive mining and railroad construction in California, as well as the coincidence that a San Francisco explosives importer was a brother of Alfred Nobel (who headed a European explosives firm) resulted in San Francisco in 1868 becoming the location for the Giant Powder Company. This, the first manufacturing plant for explosives in the United States, was followed in 1869 by the California Powder Works. Both plants, initially located in San Francisco, moved in 1879. Their not infrequent plant explosions were endangering the encroaching residential areas. The Giant Powder Company moved to Fleming Point, and then in 1892 to Giant on San Pablo Bay. The California Powder Works moved to Pinole.

In 1884 the Selby lead smelter seeking a larger site moved from San Francisco to Selby. As a result, by 1910, oil refineries, a lead smelter, a steel plant, sugar refinery, and paper and rubber works had established themselves in a coastal band stretching from Richmond to Antioch. In this area of Contra Costa County industrial growth preceded urban growth, and many of the plants had 'company towns' close by. These industries have remained to the present time, and provide the basic manufacturing character of the area.

1906—World War Two

Two major developments—the earthquake of 1906 and the

First World War—had great impact in breaking down San Francisco's industrial dominance in the first twenty years of the twentieth century. The San Francisco earthquake and fire destroyed nearly all of the central portion of San Francisco, and caused an abrupt dispersal of some 100,000 persons throughout the Bay Area. A majority of this displaced population sought refuge in the urban East Bay, and this in turn created a building boom, particularly in Oakland. Oakland's population between 1900 and 1910 increased from 66,960 to 150,174, and that of Berkeley from 13,214 to 40,434. The earthquake also resulted in the development of northern San Mateo County; by 1915 the urban area extended as far south as South San Francisco. Although San Francisco lost a large number of its inhabitants in 1906 and shortly thereafter, the city showed a population increase for the 1900–1910 decade.

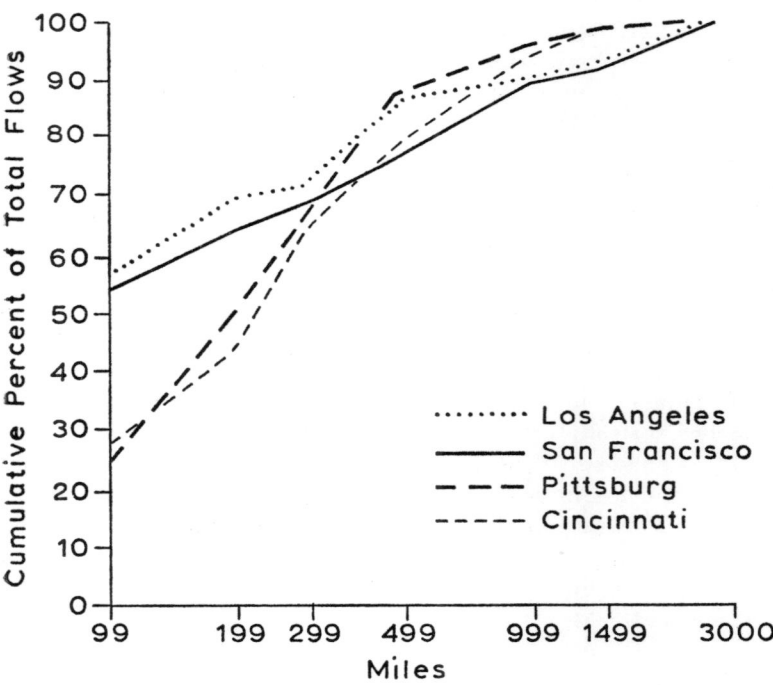

FIG. 6. TOTAL MANUFACTURING FLOWS FROM LOS ANGELES, SAN FRANCISCO, PITTSBURG, AND CINCINNATI. BASED ON 1963 CENSUS OF TRANSPORTATION DATA.

In fact, despite the earthquake and fire, the entire Bay Area experienced one of the greatest influxes of newcomers in its history, The condition of San Francisco for several years after 1906 did, however, deflect much of the new population to the suburbs.

This was a major period of expansion for the East Bay. Oakland, Berkeley and Alameda were the focus of great speculation in real estate and in transit operations. In particular, this was a period of development of a well articulated transit system for the East Bay. Certainly, by 1924, there existed a compact network of suburban transit services. The electric railway was a much more potent force for decentralization than the horsecar had been in the 1870's. Lines dependent on the horse had radiated from downtown Oakland for only three or four miles. The electric railway extended some six to twelve miles, and with its attendant real estate operations, greatly expanded the urbanized area within the limits set by the topography. In addition, there is 'strong evidence that it was relatively easy to move within the periphery, as opposed to movement in and out of the center.' (Weiss, p. 16). Beyond the city limits of San Francisco, by contrast, there were few trolley routes and the character of the metropolis was set by the railroad. In the East Bay, therefore, the clear detachment of place of residence and place of work dates from the era of the trolley. As a result, the East Bay has industrial districts like Emeryville, parts of Berkeley, East Oakland and San Leandro that date from that time. These concentrations do not represent an integration of housing and plant, as was true at Hercules, Selby and Redwood City for example, but are industrial areas to which workers commuted.

In general, industrial activity in the East Bay was largely confined to the waterfront, the largest concentration being in the Oakland portion. Emeryville had not, as of that time, the industry that was to be founded in later years, although its character as a manufacturing city had been set by 1912. Thus, by 1920, a complex of East Bay industrial districts, made possible by and tied to the well articulated transit services, challenged the predominance of San Francisco. In 1899 San Francisco had 32,555 manufacturing wage earners and the East Bay cities (Oakland, Berkeley, Alameda) 3,059. By 1919, the respective figures were 48,550 and 32,453.

Manufacturing employment in 1919 was also a reflection of the high rate of industrial activity resulting from the First World War.

This was particularly true of the shipbuilding industry which reached a peak in the period 1917 to 1921. In Oakland during that period some 140 vessels were built, compared with 21 in the 1901–1916 period, and 25 in the post-war period 1922–1931 (Hinkel, p. 876). In the Census of 1919, shipbuilding employment stood at 11,991 (24·6 per cent of total manufacturing employment) in San Francisco, and 10,855 (46·7 per cent) in Oakland.

Coincident with the beginning of World War I, the Panama Canal was opened, though it was not fully operational until 1917. The outstanding effect of the canal was to offer a competitive transportation route to the railroad between the Atlantic and Pacific seaboards. Many lines of commodities formerly using the railroad then switched to water transport. Of the westbound commodities, iron and steel, chemicals, machinery and paper used the water route to a considerable extent; eastbound, refined petroleum products and canned goods were predominant. This, in turn, increased the importance of those industrial cities of the Bay Area which possessed deepwater ports.

The World War itself threw the Bay Area very much on its own resources: intercoastal shipping was withdrawn for other more urgent needs, railroad facilities became overtaxed resulting in slow and uncertain shipments, both rail and water rates were materially increased, and eastern and middle western factories formerly supplying the area with many kinds of manufactured products were devoted to producing products necessary to the conduct of the War. During the period following the War a few industries, particularly shipbuilding and its related industries, suffered severely. Generally, the Bay Area emerged from the readjustment period with a more diversified and advanced industrial structure, partially at least in response to rapid population growth, than had existed in 1914.

By 1920 industrial employment in the Bay Area was still concentrated, but in a more dispersed form. In that year, 78 per cent of manufacturing employees were located in the seven largest cities—San Francisco, Oakland, San Jose, Alameda, Vallejo and Richmond. These concentrations were coincident with urban development at that time. The location of manufacturing employment in 1925 is shown on Figure 3. This indicates three major manufacturing concentrations: (1) San Francisco; (2) the East Bay complex of Oak-

Intrametropolitan Manufacturing Location

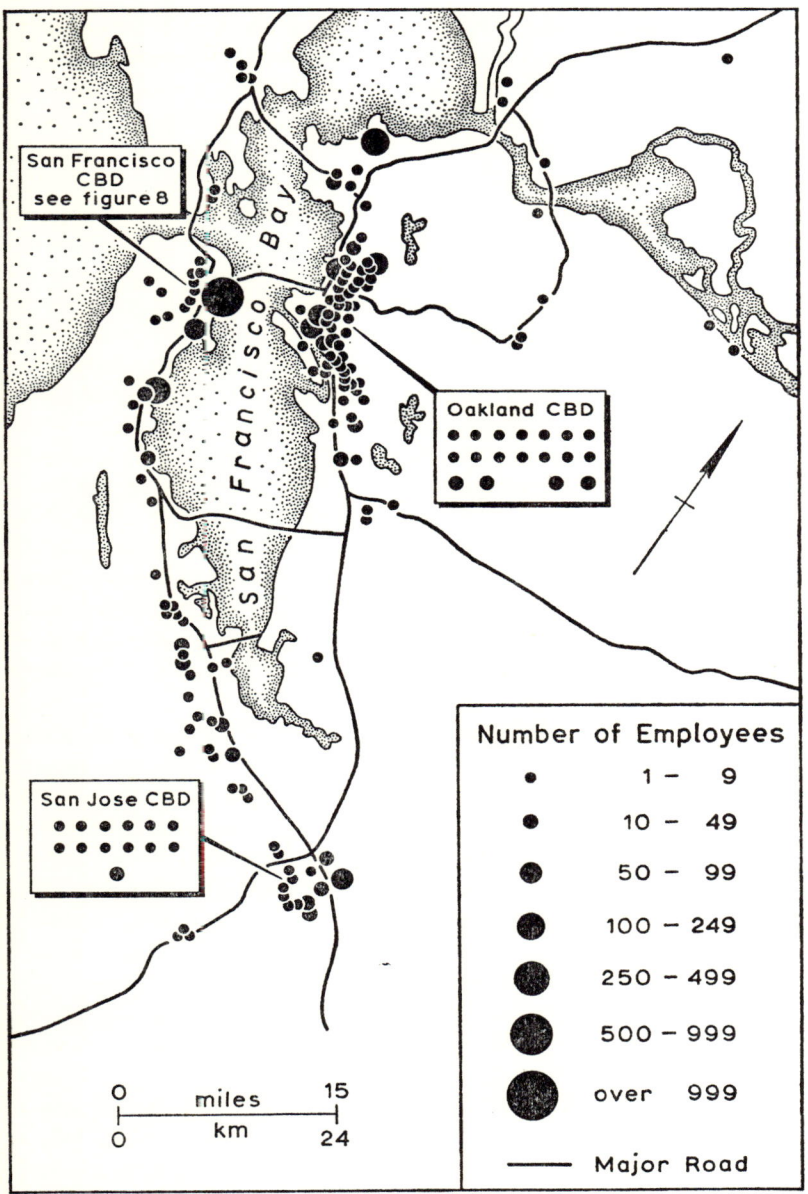

FIG. 7. LOCATION OF LETTERPRESS PRINTING PLANTS (S.I.C. 2751)—
SAN FRANCISCO BAY AREA, 1963.

land, Alameda, Emeryville and Berkeley; and (3) waterfront development following the Contra Costa county shoreline from Richmond to Pittsburgh. San Jose at this time was a minor isolated manufacturing centre. By 1963 this pattern had been radically altered by the development of the automobile and truck which provided a new dimension of freedom of location for both the industrial plant and the manufacturing employee.

The period from 1920 to 1930 was marked by a rapid increase in automobile ownership. In 1920, there were only 101,758 automobiles in the San Francisco-Oakland Metropolitan Area or 9·9 persons per automobile. By 1930, there were 358,993, or 3·8 persons per automobile. Use of motor vehicles was almost entirely local. Freight hauling by truck was also limited both in quantity and distance. Truck speeds were also low; maximum speed limits advocated in 1923 were fifteen miles per hour for trucks with solid rubber tyres and twenty-five miles per hour for those with pneumatic tyres.

The Depression and World War II produced a period of only moderate increase in automobile ownership—by 1946 there were only 524,234 automobiles in the San Francisco-Oakland Metropolitan Area—but the post-war boom and continued prosperity since catapulted automobile ownership to 1,284,759 (2·3 persons per automobile) in 1963.

Prior to World War II manufacturing in the Bay Area began to disperse from the traditional locations within the San Francisco-Oakland urban core. The tie between residential development and the rail line was broken with the increasing ownership of the automobile. 'The development of the automobile to the extent that ownership was widespread and service was dependable reached a stage around 1920 that permitted a return to the earliest orientation of transportation, that of individual rather than mass transportation. This fact freed the journey to work from the bonds of restricted mass movement along rail lines.' (Vance, 1960, p. 205). The significance of this transportation revolution to manufacturing lies in the fact that the industrial plant could draw its labour supply from a wider area (limited only by the individual worker's preference pattern) and thus tap a greater labour market in both quantitative and qualitative terms. The individual plant was thus released of any constraints previously imposed by labour supply.

Intrametropolitan Manufacturing Location

Tunnard, however, points out that this suburbanization of population could not have taken place had not home financing been made easier. He points out that high interest rates, second mortgages and other restrictions had made houses expensive for many Americans prior to 1933. The New Deal produced a government guaranteed house mortgage, and the superhighway; both factors aided suburbanization.

If the automobile rid the manufacturing plant of labour supply constraints, then the truck 'offered a new freedom to the manufacturer in selecting a site . . . and accentuated the disadvantages of the obsolescent street layout of the cities by aggravating problems of traffic congestion).' (Hoover and Vernon, p. 35). The truck, initially, was particularly important in inter-city hauls for it provided door-to-door service. The smaller unit of operation also meant the truck could perform many individual and special services for which it was more adaptable than the railroad. Thus, in the period after 1920, the erection of factories without railroad sidings became more frequent.

In the Bay Area, improvements in roads and the building of the trans-Bay bridges in the late 1930's had a direct impact on circulation and location in the area. Truck shipments replaced much of the cargo previously carried by rail, and industrial plants found it advantageous to locate at greater distances from the urban cores because of more flexible transportation facilities.

Zoning regulations, which tended to discourage the radical expansion or total replacement of plants of certain types in the central city areas and thus aided manufacturing decentralization, were introduced in the Bay Area at this time. Initial zoning regulations were imposed in San Francisco in 1921, and in Oakland in 1935.

These then were the components of the initial stages of decentralization in the 1930's. At the same time the size of the Bay Area market stimulated national corporations to develop branch plants in the area. In 1919, sixty branch plants of national concerns were located in the Bay Area, by 1929 the figure was 154, and by 1939 had reached 186. In some ways, this represents the attainment of maturity by industry in the Bay Area; national concerns crediting the Bay Area with a large and diversified enough market to make their entrance profitable.

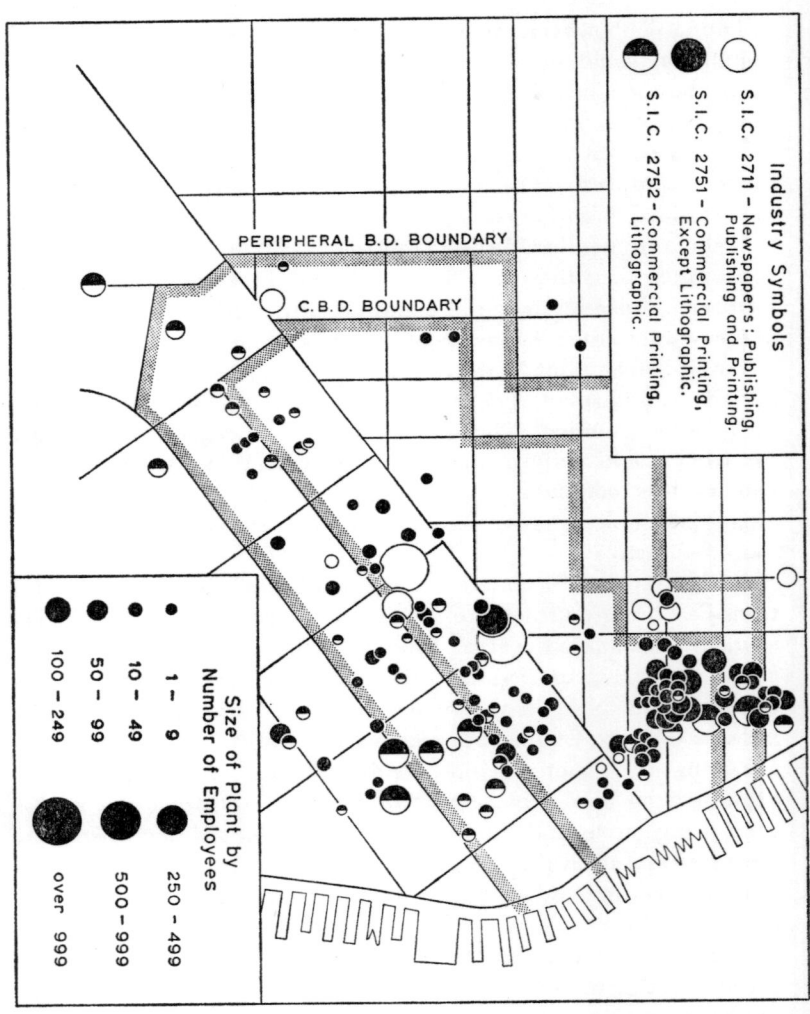

Fig. 8. Location of Letterpress Printing (S.I.C. 2751), Lithographic Printing (S.I.C. 2752), and Newspaper (S.I.C. 2711) Plants in the Central Business District Area of San Francisco, 1963.

World War II to the Present

World War II, unlike the 1914–1918 conflict, was a two front war. As a result, the Bay Area industrial base expanded rapidly to meet the demands of war. As in World War I, shipbuilding was of paramount importance. Between 1940 and 1943 a large influx of new residents moved into the Bay Area to work in shipyards, war plants and other government installations. By 1943, close to 65 per cent of the manufacturing employment in the Bay Area was engaged in shipbuilding, while manufacturing employment itself had almost tripled since 1940.

Most of the plants engaged in war production were outside the San Francisco-Oakland urban core. Four of the major locations were on the fringe of this core, namely, Richmond, Vallejo, South San Francisco and Sausalito. Richmond typifies the expansion that took place during this period. In 1940, the population of Richmond was 23,000; by 1944 it had increased to 92,000. This was a direct result of the war oriented industry of the city; shipbuilding was of major importance but Richmond also boasted of some fifty-five major war industries, producing gasoline, jeeps, tanks, troop cars and munitions. The Richmond shipyards were responsible for the production of close to 20 per cent of all Liberty and Victory ships produced by the United States during the war Vallejo, South San Francisco and Sausalito were devoted largely to shipbuilding.

After the cessation of hostilities, many of those who had initially come to the area to work in the war effort remained. This, together with the economic impetus given the area by war demands, resulted in a net addition of 55,117 manufacturing wage earners between 1939 and 1947.

Industrial expansion did not stop with the end of the war. Employment totals in manufacturing levelled off in Alameda, Contra Costa and San Francisco Counties after 1947, but San Mateo and Santa Clara Counties have continued their rapid wartime expansion to the present. These latter two counties have emerged, within the last twenty years, with an electronics and related defense industries complex. The growth of this complex accelerated rapidly after 1954, when the Lockheed Missiles and Space Plant started in Sunnyvale. With the trend to miniaturization of products in recent years, the need for assembly type operations had grown rapidly, but not nearly so rapidly as the need for research and development, partly because of the rate of obsolescence. 'The outstanding characteristics of the area's industry are the dominance

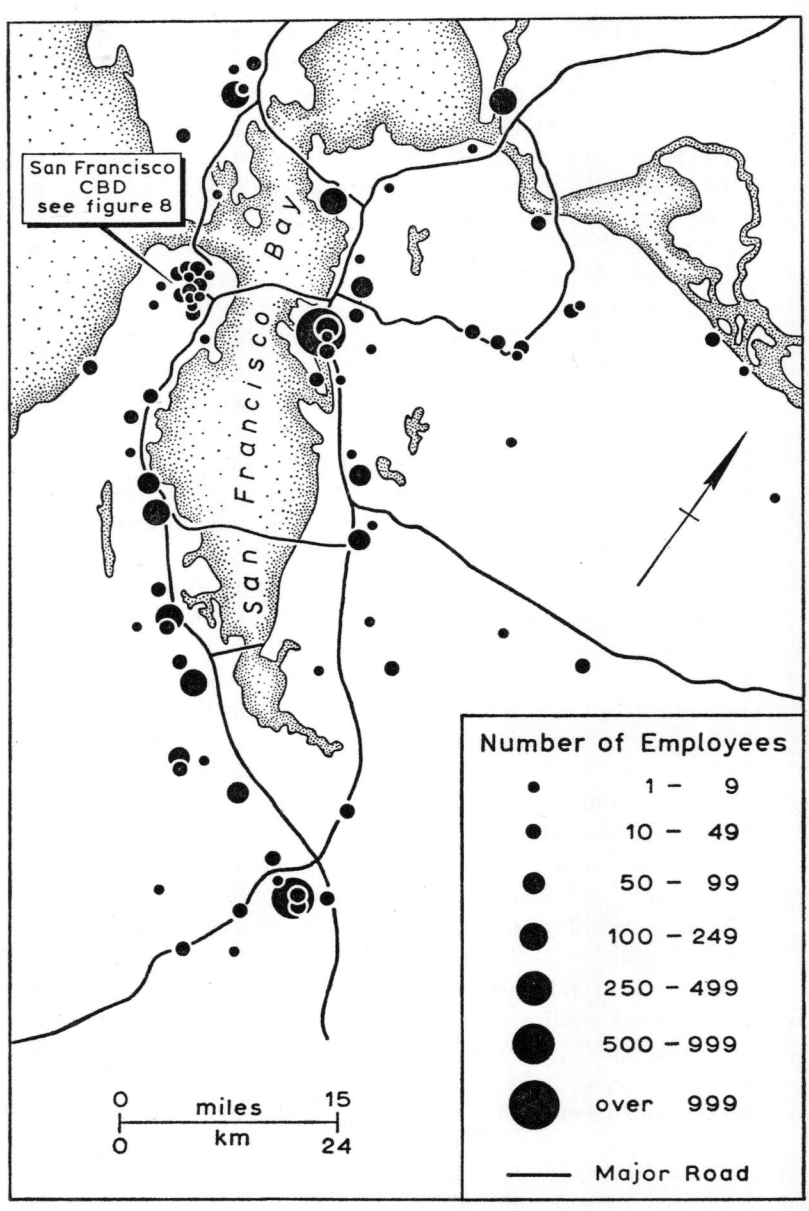

FIG. 9. LOCATION OF NEWSPAPER PLANTS (S.I.C. 2711)—
SAN FRANCISCO BAY AREA, 1963.

Intrametropolitan Manufacturing Location

of technology, the seminal role played by Stanford University, the selective attraction that the local environment had exerted on hard-to-find scientific and technical specialists and the absence of many of the problems that have plagued older areas.' (Stedman, p.35).

San Mateo and Santa Clara Counties have no monopoly on the electronics industry in the Bay Area, (of 208 electronics plants in the Bay area in 1963, Santa Clara accounted for 96, Alameda for 39, and San Mateo for 46—a total of 181 for the three counties), but they contain the heaviest concentration which is especially dense around Stanford University. The University area is the location for the Stanford Research Institute, Philco, General Electric, Varian Associates, Hewlett Packard and eighteen other electronics plants. This is the core of the electronics belt which stretches as far north as Burlingame, and as far southeast as Coyote. The area benefits from its proximity not only to Stanford University, but also to the N.A.S.A.'s Ames Laboratory and to San Francisco International Airport—for speed of delivery of the final products is often of major importance.

Farther south in Santa Clara County, the electronics firms have as their neighbours the still-important canning industry and the related container industry—tin, paper and glass all being represented. San Jose also has two large representatives of the atomic and ordnance fields—General Electric's Atomic Power Equipment Department, and FMC's Ordnance Division.

The growth of industry in Santa Clara County can best be illustrated by figures tracing the development of its three major industrial groups since 1955 (Table 4).

Traditionally Santa Clara County has been a major producer of canned and frozen foods. Until 1958, this was still the largest single industry. Employment in this industry has remained steady, however, while total manufacturing employment has increased rapidly. Between 1958 and 1966 manufacturing employment in Santa Clara County increased by 42,683, while in the entire San Francisco-Oakland Metropolitan Area the increase was only 3,925.

Basically the trend in the 1950's and the 1960's was to industries related to defence and space programmes. The two locational developments of note were the rapid growth of manufacturing in Santa Clara County, and the continuing increase in relative importance of the areas lying outside the San Francisco-East Bay

TABLE 4
MAJOR INDUSTRIES OF SANTA CLARA COUNTY, 1955–1963.

	Employment (000's)	
	1955	1963
Fruit and vegetable canning and preserving	9·8	9·2
Electrical machinery equipment and supplies	5·4	23·3
Ordnance, motor vehicles and other durable goods industries	4·5	31·9
Total 3 industries	19·7	64·4
Total all manufacturing	32·9	87·0

Source: State of California. *Division of Labour Statistics and Research.*

urban core. In 1963, there were ten additional cities compared with 1947 that had over one thousand manufacturing employees; significantly, all were outisde the San Francisco-East Bay urban core. By 1963 decentralization was a fact. However, there were some industries that clung to the established urban core. In 1963, San Francisco accounted for 87·3 per cent (by value added) of 'apparel and related products' in the Bay Area, 51·0 per cent of 'printing and publishing' and 39·3 per cent of 'furniture and fixtures.'

The map of the location of manufacturing employment in 1963 (Figure 4) is markedly different from that of 1925 (Figure 3). Industry in 1963 encircles the Bay from San Francisco to San Jose to Richmond to Pittsburg. Conspicuously there is little industry in either Marin or Solano Counties, though minor concentrations occur in San Rafael and Vallejo. The influence of topography is also very apparent in that industrial activity clings to the flatter shoreline areas of the Bay itself. With development continuing at a rapid rate, there is little reason to doubt that the interstices of this pattern will be filled in, topography permitting, in the years ahead.

From 1958 to 1961 some 917 new plants were established in the Bay Area (Table 5).

TABLE 5
NEW PLANTS IN THE SAN FRANCISCO BAY AREA 1958–1961

	No. of new plants established	Percentage of new plants with investment below $50,000
East Bay Cities (Alameda, Oakland, Emeryville, Berkeley)	220	77·7
San Francisco	183	90·7
Santa Clara	169	62·1
San Mateo	133	84·2
Alameda County minus East Bay Cities	117	54·7
Contra Costa	65	75·4
Marin	25	72·0
Solano	0	100·0
	917	

(Note: no data available post-1961.)
Source: *New Plants and Expansions*, annual publication of the San Francisco Chamber of Commerce.

This table suggests that much of the investment in the old urban core (San Francisco and the East Bay Cities) was in small replacement enterprises, loft occupying plants, etc., which had relatively little impact on overall industrial structure or growth. Conversely, the high percentage of plants with an investment of $50,000 plus in Santa Clara County and the remainder of Alameda County strengthens the evidence pointing to these areas as the growth foci at the present time.

Decentralization of manufacturing away from the older central cities—San Francisco and Oakland—appears to be a continuing process in the Bay Area. Manufacturing employment in San Francisco decreased by 4,660 between 1958 and 1963, and in Oakland by 3,441 in the same period. This is in contrast to the other, but 'newer,' major metropolitan centre of San Jose which experienced a growth of 3,483 manufacturing employees in the 1958 to 1963 period. In the older central cities, plants have become cramped for space or obsolete, and employers have deserted their loft-type buildings and relocated in the surrounding industrial parks in single story buildings. However, more than compensating for these losses has been an office building boom to house expanding company headquarters and financial institutions. As a result, San Francisco is becoming more specialized in its financial, service and administrative functions vis-a-vis the total Bay Area complex. Manufacturing and wholesale trade have thus suburbanized; in general the degree of manufacturing suburbanization in the Bay Area exceeds that of most other metropolitan areas in the nation, although it is less than in other California metropolitan areas.

In terms of their 'employment fields,' the two major urban centres of San Francisco and Oakland stand apart from each other. This is illustrated by the following table, which shows the Counties, and parts of Counties, from which San Francisco and Oakland draw their employment.

Table 6 indicates that 89·9 per cent of San Francisco's employment is drawn from the 'employment field' lying west of the Bay; similarly, 96·7 per cent of Oakland's employment is drawn from east of the Bay. It would appear therefore that each 'unit' operates in a relatively independent way; 'this generalization is basically valid, and quite specifically so with respect to the functions that Oakland and San Francisco share.' (Vance, 1964, p. 84).

In any analysis of Bay Area manufacturing, therefore, a recognition of this dichotomy should be made. The central cities are San Francisco and Oakland, each of approximately equal importance to its respective employment field. San Jose, because of its more recent growth, does not fit this pattern so readily and must

TABLE 6

SAN FRANCISCO AND OAKLAND EMPLOYMENT FIELDS, 1960

San Francisco Employees	72·4% reside in San Francisco
	13·2% reside in San Mateo County
	4·3% reside in Marin County
	3·0% reside in Alameda County (less Oakland)
	2·7% reside in Oakland
	2·3% reside in Contra Costa County
Oakland Employees	58·6% reside in Oakland
	28·9% reside in Alameda County (less Oakland)
	9·2% reside in Contra Costa County
	1·8% reside in San Francisco

Source: Wallace F. Smith, *Housing Market Data from Census Materials. A Study of California and the Bay Area.* (Berkeley, 1963), page 60.

be treated separately and as a distinctive case. In addition, recognition must be made of the high degree of decentralization of manufacturing that has occurred concomitantly with the suburbanization of population. Thus the existence of non-central city employment fields, for which no data is available, should be recognized.

CHAPTER III

A Typology of Intrametropolitan Manufacturing Location

This study can claim two distinct advantages over previous attempts to analyse intrametropolitan manufacturing location. First, it is based on the collection of a substantial amount of data on each of the twenty-three selected industries (Table 7), with regard both to general features and to specific characteristics within the San Francisco Bay Area. Second, the plants in each separate industry have been mapped by street address and plant size so that a set of maps of selected disaggregated industries for the study area has been produced.

On the basis of the data collected, the following characteristics were isolated as being most discriminating in terms of locational analysis.

1. *Location Pattern*

For purposes of analysis a series of sub-areas within the San Francisco Bay Area was established. These were 'urban clusters,' 'traditional urban core areas,' 'Central Business Districts,' and 'Peripheral Business Districts.'* By means of a simple analysis of concentration in each of these sub-divisions different location patterns are recognizable. In addition to the above sub-areas, recognition is also made of the possibility of an industry (or group of industries) being strongly concentrated outside of all the above areas; a number of electronics industries in the Bay Area, for example, exhibit location patterns of this type.

---

*Three *urban clusters* were designated, (i) *San Francisco* (consisting of San Francisco and Daly City); (ii) *Oakland* (Oakland, Alameda, Emeryville, Berkeley, and San Leandro); and (iii) *San Jose* (San Jose, Santa Clara, and Sunnyvale). Two *traditional urban cores*, (i) *San Francisco* (consisting solely of San Francisco County) and (ii) *Oakland* (Oakland, Alameda, Emeryville, and Berkeley). The Central Business Districts of San Francisco, Oakland, and San Jose are as delineated in the 1954 *Census of Business*. The Peripheral Business Districts of San Francisco, Oakland, and San Jose are two block wide 'frame', areas surrounding the designated Central Business Districts.

Intrametropolitan Manufacturing Location

SELECTED INDUSTRIES OF THE SAN FRANCISCO BAY AREA, 1962.

S.I.C.	Industry Description	Employment[1]	Total No. of Plants[2]	Number of Sample Plants[3]	Number of Sample Plants Classified as Local
2026	Fluid Milk	4,196	50	15	14
2051	Bread and Related Products	5,790	99	23	20
2711	Newspapers	8,460	107	22	21
2751	Printing: Letterpress	3,987	278	40	36
2752	Printing: Lithographic	3,803	100	28	23
3221	Glass Containers	2,675	6	4	4
3411	Metal Cans	4,099	18	10	9
3441	Fabricated Structural Steel	2,768	38	22	9
3731	Ship Building and Repairing	5,587	14	6	6
2033	Canned Fruit and Vegetables	12,698	55	29	2
2071	Candy (Sweets and Confectionery)	3,345	44	15	2
2082	Malt Liquor	2,456	5	4	1
2851	Paints and Varnishes	2,185[4]	66	16	8
2911	Petroleum Refining	6,770	6	5	0
3312	Blast Furnaces and Steel Mills	5,761	4	2	1
3571	Computing and Accounting Machines	5,115	8	6	0
3611	Electric Measuring Instruments	4,055	16	11	2
3673	Tungsten, Electronic Tubes	4,580	9	7	0
3679	Electronic Products, n.e.c.	3,190	47	14	3
3711	Motor Vehicles	4,756	6	5	1
1925	Guided Missiles, etc.	} 21,290[5]			
1931	Tanks and Tank Components		4	3	0
3511	Steam Engines				
	TOTAL	118,051	981	287	162

[1]*Census of Manufactures*: 1958; [2]1962; [3]Number of Plants for which questionnaire data available; [4]Industry included on the basis of "value added" criterion; [5]Industries analysed as a group because of 'disclosure' problems.

2. Market Area Served

The starting point for past classifications of industries on the basis of market area served has usually been a differentiation between those industries serving local and those serving non-local markets. The work of both Pred and De Meirlier embraces this position, though it should be noted that Pred recognizes the effect of regional and national markets on industrial location patterns within the general non-local market category. It is relatively easy to give examples of industries which fall into either local or non-local market categories. However, the categorizing of a series of industries is a more difficult task. One conclusion reached by this study is that no clear division exists between local market serving and non-local market serving industries: the division is confused because of the heterogenous nature of some of the industries, past allocation decisions, the range of plant sizes in any one industry, and the fact that similar location patterns may embrace both of these somewhat simple market area distinctions*. Rather there is a range of market sizes for industries, and sometimes for different plants within the same industry, which stretches from totally local at one end of the spectrum to largely national at the other. It should be noted that some industries, particularly at seaport locations, are aimed at international markets.

This problem can be partially overcome by classifying industries into categories which embrace adjacent levels of a market hierarchy. The suggested market hierarchy is a simple one of three levels—local, regional, and multi-regional or national (Figure 5). This is in line with the categorization suggested by Duncan drawing upon the earlier work of McKenzie. Duncan's classification of 'areas related to the metropolis' is threefold. 'Area A' corresponds to the 'Metropolitan area' concept of McKenzie; operationally it is simply the SMA itself. 'Area B' corresponds to McKenzie's 'trade area' based on Federal Reserve Districts and newspaper circulation . . . 'Area C' is a residual category in the classification,

---

*Wedervang has made the relevant observation that 'when an industry has reached a stage of maturity producing a complex of products, there is likely to be a specialization between large establishments concentrating on mass production, medium size establishments which specialize in certain products at an efficient scale, and small establishments which fill the gaps by performing special jobs, such as repair jobs, taking rush orders, etc'. Wedervang p. 77.

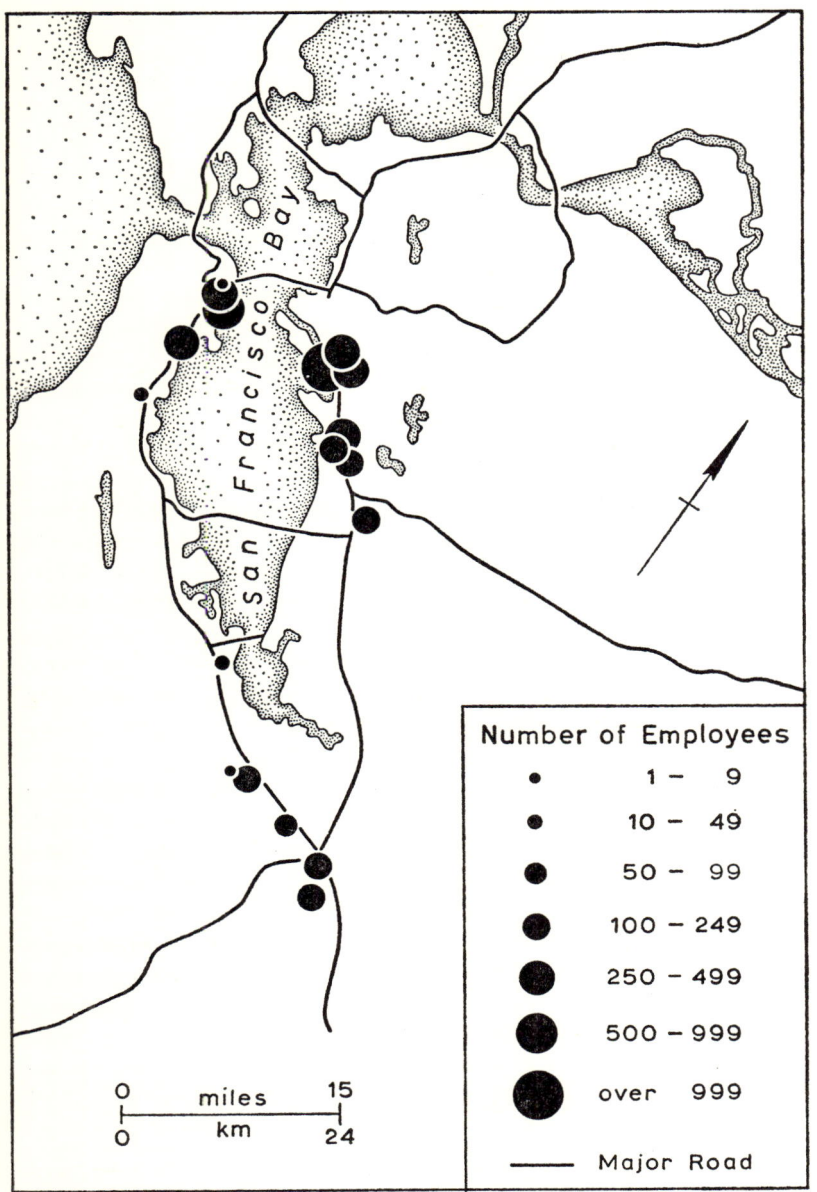

FIG. 10. LOCATION OF METAL CAN PLANTS (S.I.C. 3411)—
SAN FRANCISCO BAY AREA, 1963.

TABLE 8

PERCENTAGE OF SHIPMENTS (TONS) BY SELECTED FLOW DISTANCES FOR LOS ANGELES, SAN FRANCISCO, PITTSBURGH, CINCINNATI AND THE UNITED STATES, 1963

	Short		Shipment Distances Intermediate	Long
	0–99	0–199	200–1499	1500 plus
San Francisco	54·2	64·5	26·4	9·1
Los Angeles	57·3	69·5	21·0	9·5
Pittsburgh	26·8	49·1	48·1	2·8
Cincinnati	28·1	43·4	53·4	3·2
U.S.A.	30·0	45·6	49·3	5·1

Source: *1963 Census of Transportation*.

embracing all origins and destinations not fairly clearly localized in 'Areas A or B'. (Duncan, p. 232). For the Bay Area, the local market ('Area A') is simply the San Francisco-Oakland and San Jose S.M.S.A.'s; the outer limits of the regional market are set, somewhat arbitrarily, at 300 miles on the basis of aporoximately half the distance to the nearest competing centres at the same hierarchical level, namely Portland, Salt Lake City, and Los Angeles;* and the multi-regional designation is given to all market areas larger than that of the single region.

It should be recognized that because of the relatively low accessibility of the Bay Area to the national market, manufacturing flows from the Bay Area differ markedly from the national averages and from those metropolitan areas located in the Manufacturing Belt (for example, Cincinnati and Pittsburgh) but are similar to those for metropolitan areas with low accessibility (for example, Los Angeles). Data obtained from the 1963 *Census of Transportation* on total manufacturing flows for San Francisco, Los Angeles, Cincinnati, and Pittsburgh are plotted in Figure 6. The most striking differences are in short and long flows, as Table 8 indicates. This supports the theoretically based contention of Pred

---

*The distance chosen allows the use of *Census of Transportation* data which breaks its shipment figures at 99, 199, 299, 499, 999, 1499, and 1500 plus mile levels. Of the alternatives presented by these data, the 299 mile break is considered the most relevant in terms of designating a regional market.

TABLE 9

CLASSIFICATION OF INDUSTRIES BASED ON SITE REQUIREMENTS PER PLANT AND PER PRODUCTION EMPLOYEE. SAN FRANCISCO BAY AREA, 1963.

		Site Area (Sq. Feet)	
		Per Plant	Per Production Employee
Large Per Plant and Per Employee			
S.I.C.	Industry		
2911	Petroleum Refining	3,650,728	4,487
1925	Guided Missiles	⎫	
1931	Tanks and Tank Components	⎬ 1,285,020	301
3511	Steam Engines	⎭	
3711	Motor Vehicles	553,352	457
3571	Computing and Accounting	266,073	347
3312	Blast Furnace and Steel Mills	178,596	396
3731	Ship Building	134,383	364
Medium Per Plant and Per Employee			
S.I.C.	Industry		
2033	Canned Fruit and Vegetables	80,854	268
3221	Glass Containers	69,000	220
2082	Malt Liquor	59,866	212
3679	Electronic Products, n.e.c.	51,838	140
3411	Metal Cans	49,146	215
3673	Tungsten: Electronic Tubes	44,419	109
3611	Electric Measuring Instruments	34,388	112
2851	Paints and Varnishes	24,479	507*
3441	Fabricated Structural Steel	22,280	382*
2026	Fluid Milk	10,926	238
Small Per Plant and Per Employee			
S.I.C.	Industry		
2051	Bread and Related Products	7,743	110
2071	Candy	6,667	88
2752	Printing: Lithographic	5,869	88
2751	Printing: Letterpress	3,785	131
2711	Newspapers	2,905	28

*Large Site Area Per Production Employee

Source: Questionnaire Returns, 1963.

that 'short flows catering to nearby markets will predominate in low-accessibility areas and in some well populated areas, as in California, will attain considerable proportions. However, because of the attractive force exercised by the large percentage of the national or regional market concentrated in the high accessibility area, as well as the prevalence of tapering freight rate structures, a larger percentage of long-distance hauls will characterize low-accessibility areas, . . . ' (Pred, 1964b, p. 74). Low accessibility areas, therefore, have a relatively small intermediate flow component. In the San Francisco Bay Area the effect of this is to make those regional market industries that fall into the 'Local/Regional' (or lower half of the 'Regional') market classification have a stronger local market component than the national average. For example, at the national level only 25·7 per cent of the output (by tonnage) of the paints and varnishes industry is distributed to points within ninety-nine miles of the production area; for the San Francisco Bay Area the percentage is 45·5. The same is true of the petroleum refining industry (San Francisco 62·5 per cent compared with the national figure of 26·9 per cent within the ninety-nine mile limit) and the electric measuring instrument industry (San Francisco 28·6 per cent, U.S.A. 8·5 per cent).

Conversely, those regional market industries that fall into the 'Regional/Multi-Regional' and upper half of the 'Regional' categories have a smaller local, and a larger long flow, component than the national average. The electronics products industry at the national level distributes 19·3 per cent of its products up to ninety-nine miles and only 10 per cent over 1500 miles. The comparable figures for San Francisco are 13·4 per cent and 69·5 per cent. Similarly, the canned fruit and vegetable industry at the national level distributes 13·9 per cent of its products up to ninety-nine miles and 13·4 per cent over 1500 miles. Comparable statistics for San Francisco are 7·4 per cent and 67·3 per cent.*

The size of the market of the individual plant is relevant in the case of certain industries. Smaller plants generally serve a more restricted market, particularly in those industries where the product is perishable or extremely bulky, and in which small scale operation is possible. In some of these industries, the central city establish-

---

*All figures are obtained from the *1963 Census of Transportation*.

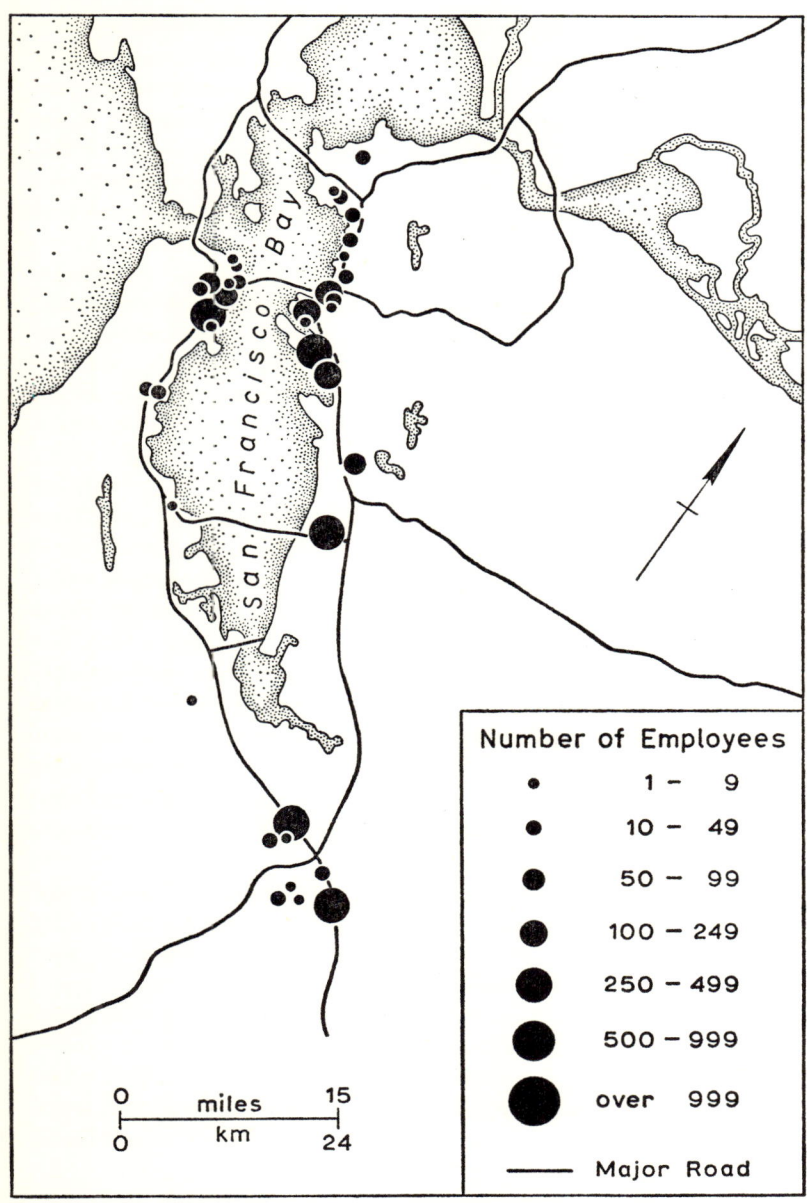

Fig. 11. Location of Fabricated Structural Steel Plants (S.I.C. 3441)—San Francisco Bay Area, 1963.

ments are the largest. In these cases the market served is either the whole, or a large part of the total, metropolitan market, and in such industries accessibility to that market is deemed critical. Other plants serving regional markets, as for example motor vehicle assembly, will attempt to locate in order to reduce transportation costs and back hauling. This, in turn, may produce a location pattern concentrated on the side of the metropolitan area facing the major part of the regional market.

This factor also includes the necessity of looking at linkages as they may exist between plants (and industries) and the type of market they serve, that is whether the market is primarily composed of wholesalers, retailers, or manufacturers. Many industries are linked to other manufacturers and, possibly because of the nature of their products, have to be spatially close to that manufacturer.

3. *Plant Characteristics*

This term covers such factors as site area required per plant and per employee, length of plant occupance, and the characteristics of the building occupied by a plant (multi or single story, and whether built specifically for the company occupying the building).

The degree of attraction exerted by the urban core areas can be measured against the degree to which an industry can (on the basis of site requirement) afford a location close to an urban core location. There are then two factors working in opposite directions: cost of land and site requirement. The cost of land generally increases toward the centre of the urban core areas.

The high cost of land in the more concentrated commercial and industrial areas is combined with a relative lack of available land; together these factors may preclude the building there of large acreage manufacturing establishments. On the basis of space requirements alone it has been stated that 'an industry requiring much space per plant and per employee could expect to find a suitable location only in those parts of the Region away from urban areas, where land is cheap and not in general demand. Industries requiring little space per employee would seem free to locate in or close to intensively developed urban areas.' (Lowry, p. 64). On the basis of data collected through questionnaires, the industries selected for study can be categorized with respect to that criterion (Table 9).

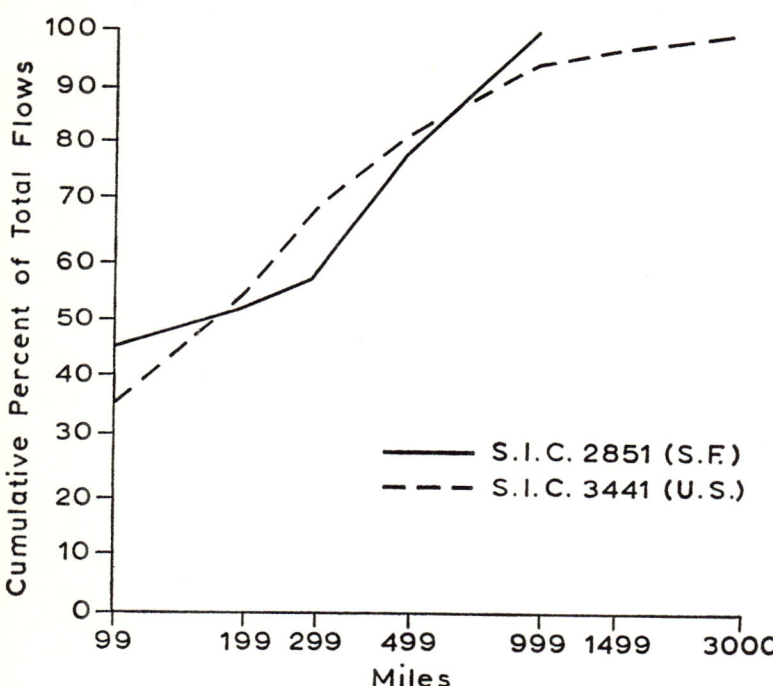

FIG. 12. MANUFACTURING FLOWS FOR THE PAINTS AND VARNISHES (S.I.C. 2851) AND FABRICATED STRUCTURAL STEEL (S.I.C. 3441) INDUSTRIES BASED ON 1963 CENSUS OF TRANSPORTATION DATA.

Note: In this and subsequent figures of the same type, the letters in parentheses indicate whether flows are based on national data (U.S.) or San Francisco Production Area data (S.F.)

There has, of course, been an outward shift of many industries from central city locations in a search for more space. 'It has not been simply a question of finding more factory room for more machines; such a need could be provided in many cases by adding a floor or two to existing factory structures.' (Hoover and Vernon, p. 27). It is rather that the structures themselves are no longer of the right type. Today, the common practice in many lines of industry is to 'find a site which imposes the least possible restraint on the shape of the structure; to plan a production layout suitable for modern processes; and then to wrap a building in a majority of cases a single storey structure around the layout.' The New York Metropolitan Study provides some data on this subject. A survey of average space used in 1956 in 239 plants showed that pre-1922 plants stood on 1040 square feet of plot space per worker, while plants built between 1922 and 1945 occupied 2000 square feet and those built after 1945 occupied 4550 square feet of plot space per worker (Hoover and Vernon, p. 27).

The returned questionnaires from plants in the Bay Area provide data which shed some light on the flexibility of an industry's building requirements, and the degree to which this has affected plant location patterns in the long term. Data were collected concerning the nature of buildings and the number of years a firm has occupied a given building.

Some industries, noticeably those with non-specialized plant requirements, can draw upon existing 'stocks' of buildings within the metropolitan area. These fall into two general categories. First, those industries that require a downtown location and are of small enough scale to be able to operate effectively in 'loft' space. Examples of such industries are lithographic and letterpress printing and women's apparel. Second, industries, usually of much larger scale than those occupying 'loft' space, which are able to use older, relatively adaptable, and relatively inexpensive, floor space. These industries can often find such space, for example, in the wholesaling districts of the older urban centres, or in the traditional industrial waterfront areas. Such industries in the Bay Area are the bread, candy, and fabricated structural steel industries.

4. *Transportation Media Used*

Some forms of transportation, such as railroad and water, are fixed at any given moment of time, and are limited in the area of a region that they can directly serve. Even allowing for the construction of spur lines, for example, the railroad can only serve a limited section of the Bay Area directly, though the use of freight forwarders may serve to overcome this to some extent. As Hoover has pointed out, 'trains are large transport units, particularly adapted to transportation in bulk; consequently they favour the concentration of production in large plants.' (Hoover, p. 169).

Hoover argues, therefore, that the railroad is especially significant for interregional specialization. The railroad plays an increasingly important role as the size of plant increases. Pegrum indicates that of plants in Los Angeles employing 500 or more persons 61 per cent had railroad sidings, in plants employing 250–499 persons 43 per cent had railroad sidings, and for the 100–249 and 50–99 employment categories the respective figures were 30 and 17 per cent. (Pegrum, p. 35).

Only plants located in limited areas in the Bay Area can consider procuring raw materials or distributing their final products by water. Additional limitations are imposed with respect to depth of channel, and whether a wharf is being shared (as in a general cargo port) or whether the plant is large enough to have its own waterfront facilities. The shipbuilding and petroleum refining industries are particularly sensitive to factors such as those outlined above.

It should be noted that generally water and rail play a far larger role in bringing 'raw materials' into plants than they do in the final distribution of products. There is, however, a greater proclivity for large plants distributing to national or regional markets (for example, the canned fruit and vegetable industry) to use rail for final distribution.

The fixed and limited nature of water and rail transportation are relevant constraints in terms of movement of goods and materials in an urban area. To this, however, should be added the factor of speed of delivery. Some industrial plants possessing railroad sidings do not use them, preferring faster forms of transportation. Such faster forms are of both a limited form (there are, for example, only a limited number of airports able to handle freight in any metropolitan area), and of a more flexible form (the truck). The medium of transportation has a greater influence on metropolitan location patterns than the origin of the inputs to the industry. Thus, rather than distinugish between location patterns on the basis of the local or national origin of raw materials, as did De Meirlier, this study considers the transportation media used to collect inputs and distribute output of greater importance.

In terms of analysing intrametropolitan patterns of industrial location, therefore, the use of railroad sidings, water transportation, and pipelines are much more locationally constraining (other things being equal) than the use of truck transportation.

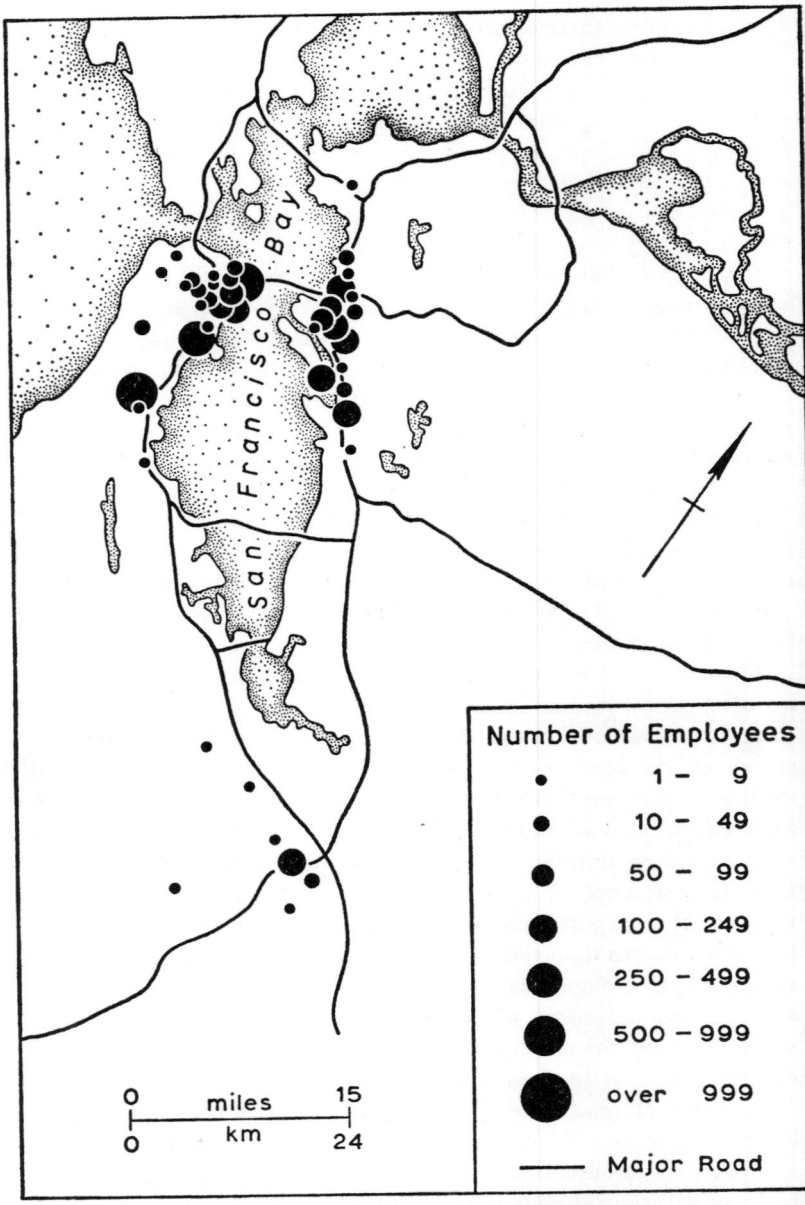

Fig. 13. LOCATION OF CANDY (SWEETS AND CONFECTIONERY) PLANTS (S.I.C. 2071)—SAN FRANCISCO BAY AREA, 1963.

5. *Nature of Product and/or Raw Materials*

In some industries the product or major raw material is perishable or extremely bulky (with low value per unit of weight), and as such the industry is drawn to either a market location (in the case of a final product) or to a raw material location (in the case of a perishable raw material input). In the Bay Area, the metal can and and glass container industries are examples of the former, and the canned fruit and vegetable industry is an example of the latter.

6. *Communication Orientation*

Industries responsive to 'communication economies' are highly concentrated in terms of location, often in the centre of a metropolitan region. For this reason, they form a distinctive group. In addition, their products are understandardized, the plants comprising the industry are relatively small, and there is a need for communication (usually rapid) between the component parts of the industry and between producer and consumer prior to production. Such industries as commercial printing, lithographing, women's apparel, and certain electronic industries fall into this group.

On the basis of the above set of six characteristics, thirteen distinct intrametropolitan manufacturing locations are recognized; these are grouped by market area types.

A. *LOCAL MARKET SERVING INDUSTRIES*

These industries are classified as serving a local market entirely on the evidence of the questionnaire data collected. The *Census of Transportation* data are of no direct use, because they deliberately exclude 'local shipments.' As a result, a number of industries included in this study (S.I.C. 2051—Bread and Related Products; S.I.C. 2026—Fluid Milk; and S.I.C. 27—Printing, Publishing, and Allied Products) are excluded from the *Census of Transportation* because 'their products . . . were distributed primarily to local markets.' (U.S. Bureau of Census, p. *vii*). There are a total of 119 sampled plants in this local market group. Some 107 of these served a local market, while the remaining twelve served a non-local market; of the latter group, however, nine (75 per cent) employed in excess of 100 persons.

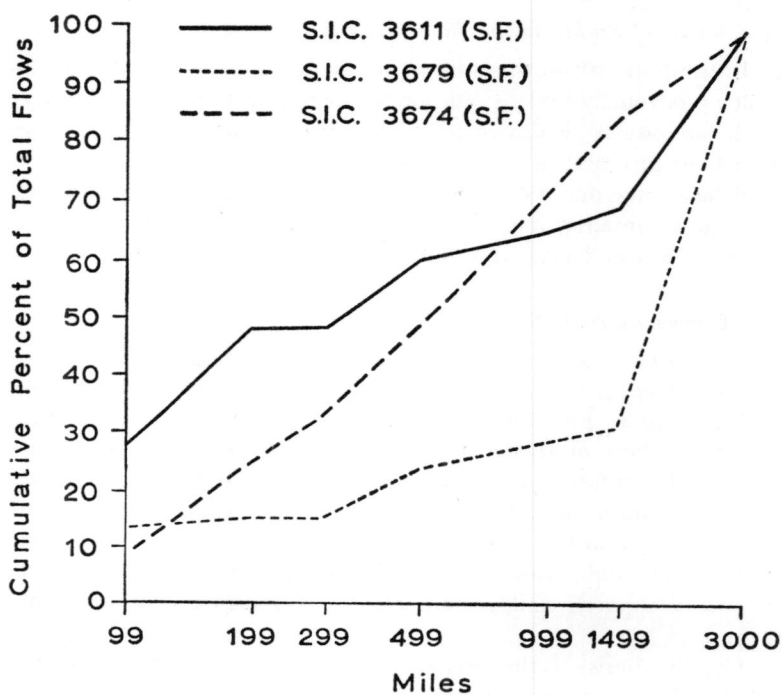

Fig. 14. Manufacturing Flows for the Motor Vehicles (S.I.C. 3711), Blast Furnaces and Steel Mills (S.I.C. 3312), and Malt Liquor (S.I.C. 2082) Industries based on 1963 Census of Transportation data.

A.1. *Central Business District Concentrated. Communication Oriented.* Industries S.I.C. 2751—Printing: Letterpress (Figure 7), and S.I.C. 2752—Printing: Lithographic.

These industries are strongly attached to the three urban clusters: some 68 per cent of the total of 378 plants in these two printing industries are found in such locations. Within these urban clusters, however, there is a strong association with the Central Business Districts (C.B.D.'s) and the Peripheral Business Districts (P.B.D.'s) surrounding them; of the 257 plants located in the urban clusters, some 178 are located in these areas. The micro-locational pattern is different as between the large (employing 100 or more persons) and the small plants. Among the large plants 46 per cent are located in the C.B.D. or P.B.D., while among the small plants the figure is 47 per cent. However, there are three and one half as many small plants in the C.B.D. as in the P.B.D., while there are twice as many large plants in the P.B.D. as in the C.B.D. This is an indication of the pressure for space in the C.B.D., and the fact that while the small plant can survive in a loft building, the large plant is likely to require an entire building or large part of a building. The total concentration of both industries in the central city areas of Oakland and San Francisco is quite marked and is the outstanding locational characteristic (Figure 8). Concentration in these downtown areas also brings with it certain disadvantages; 'the higher cost of getting to and from a central location because of congestion on the streets, and the higher cost of handling freight at the plant because of inadequate facilities.' (Chinitz, p. 145).

The two industries comprising this group are strongly local market oriented. Sixty-eight questionnaire respondents indicated that fifty-nine of them served a local market, and, of the nine exceptions, eight employed in excess of 100 persons.

The site space per plant and per employee is small, which gives this industry group the potential, in this case realized, to locate well within the urban core areas. Most of the firms occupy plants not built for them specifically; 64 per cent of all plants fit this category. Most of the plants (59 per cent) are in multi-storey buildings. In addition, a significant number of the plants (24 per cent) are of long-term (pre-1940) occupance. The larger plants are more likely to operate in single storey buildings built specifically for them. This, of course, results from the requirements for larger tracts of land upon which to build and long-run standardized production characteristics (which reduces the necessity for a central city location), and produces a more dispersed location pattern.

These industries are major users of truck transportation; local market distribution is almost entirely by this medium, with minor amounts of the product being distributed by motorcycle, hand, and parcel post. Truck is again dominant with respect to inputs, though rail with freight forwarder is a significant minor carrier. Only eight of the sixty-eight sample plants have railroad sidings, and six of these are large plants who presumably are able to operate at a larger scale making the use of rail more likely.

Besides being strongly local market oriented, these industries serve a strongly concentrated market, that is the downtown legal,

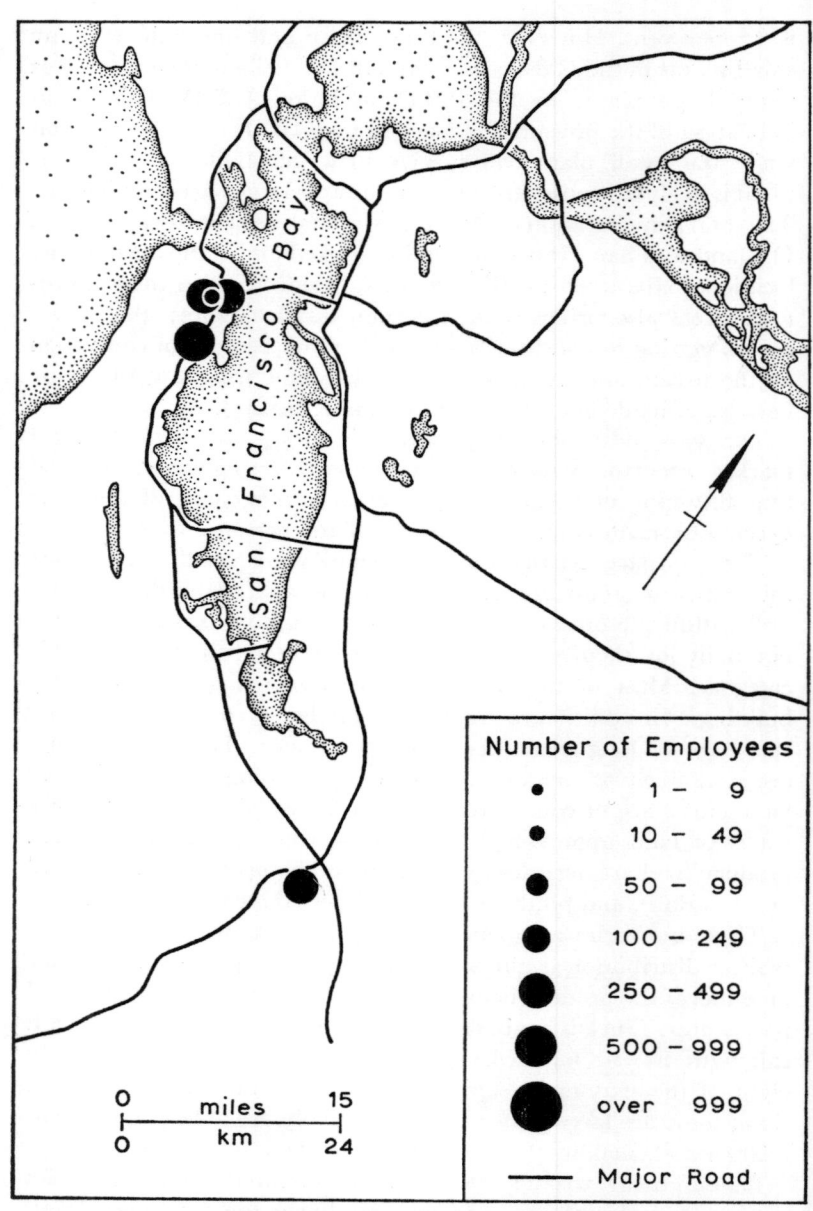

Fig. 15. LOCATION OF MALT LIQUOR PLANTS (S.I.C. 2082)—
SAN FRANCISCO BAY AREA, 1963.

administrative, and financial establishments. The close spatial tie between this concentrated market and these industries results from the necessity for rapid communication, plus the advantages to be obtained from the adjacent location of sub-contractors and supply houses of various types; that is from so-called 'external economies.'

A.2. *Dispersed Location Pattern but Large Plants Urban Core Oriented. General Consumer Market.* Industries S.I.C. 2711—Newspapers (Figure 9), and S.I.C. 2026—Fluid Milk.

Both of these industries are highly dispersed in the San Francisco Bay Area. While the degree of concentration of plants in the urban clusters is 49 per cent (76 of a total of 157 plants), roughly similar to the degree of population concentration, in the traditional urban core areas it was only 38 per cent (population concentration 46 per cent).

The newspaper industry shows a degree of C.B.D. orientation (12 of 107 plants are located in C.B.D.'s), while the fluid milk industry displays no such pattern. The answer lies in the fact that the newspaper industry is really a two-fold industry, composed of the large circulation dailies with sub-metropolitan market areas and the remainder which serve small market areas. The former group is the one that seeks C.B.D. locations, partly in the belief that this reduces costs of distribution and partly to be at the news centre of the metropolitan area. Thus the twelve plants in C.B.D. locations include the five largest plants in the Bay Area newspaper industry. These five plants, in turn, produce the six largest circulation dailies. The remainder of the newspaper plants are highly dispersed and serve rather small market areas. The fluid milk industry, of course, also has large plants and these show a propensity to locate in the major urban centres; of the eleven large plants, seven are in the traditional urban core areas centred on San Francisco and Oakland.

Both industries are strongly local market oriented. Thirty-seven plants responded to the questionnaire, and thirty-five of those indicated that they primarily served a local market. The attachment to the local market results from the nature of the product, and in the case of fluid milk the raw material as well. The products of both industries are perishable commodities; old newspaper news has as little value as spoiled milk. Thus there is the need to be as close to the majority of the final consumers as possible.

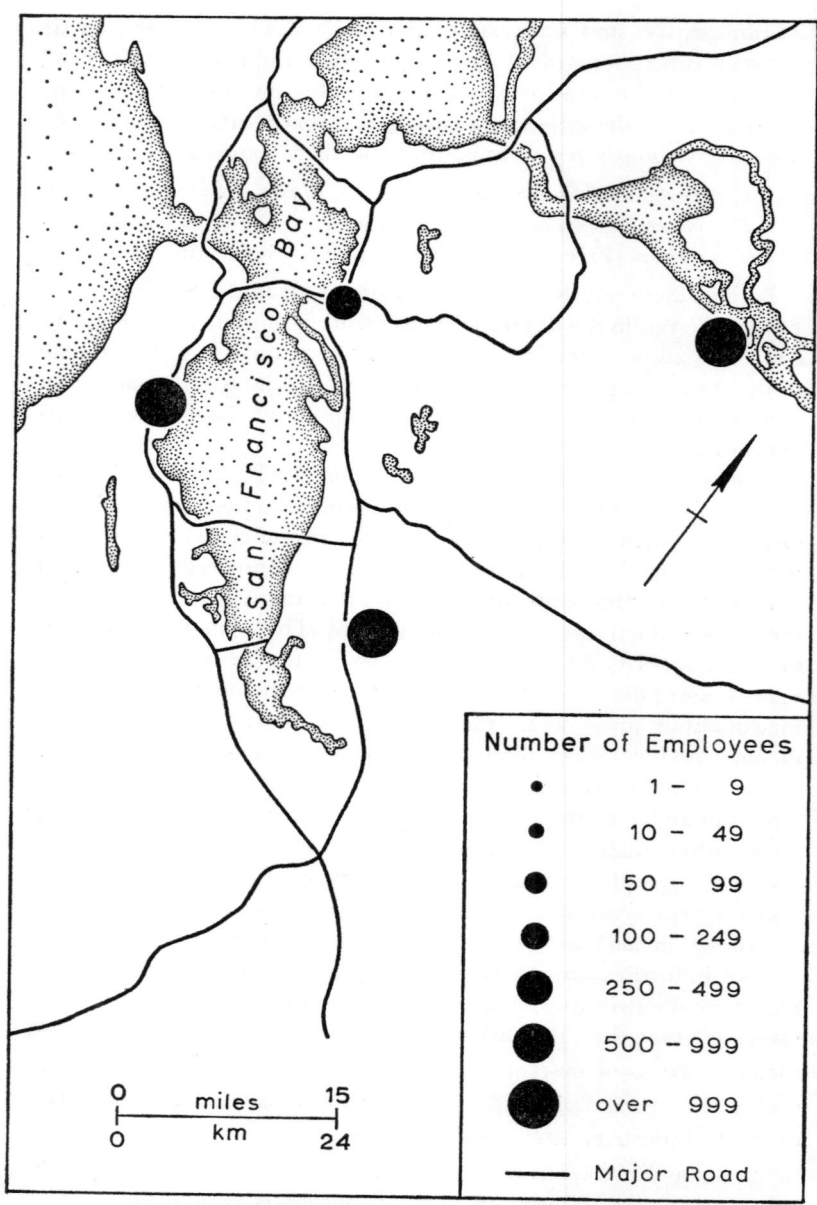

Fig. 16. Location of Blast Furnaces and Steel Mills (S.I.C. 3312) San Francisco Bay Area, 1963.

The site area required per plant and per employee is low in each industry; both industries rank in the lowest five of the twenty-three selected industries. For the majority of plants, however, centrality of location with respect to the total Bay Area is irrelevant, though centrality of location to their particular small and limited market area is important.

Plants in these industries are strongly dependent upon truck transportation. To both the local and non-local markets, truck distribution is used in almost all cases, the few divergencies being accounted for by the mail distribution of newspapers. In terms of inputs of materials, truck again is dominant with the railroad being of minor importance in both industries. The industry type is, therefore, not constrained by fixed lines of transportation.

A.3. *Bulky Product. Linked to Local Manufacturer.* Industries S.I.C. 3221—Glass Containers, and S.I.C. 3411—Metal Cans (Figure 10).

The dominant feature of these industries is that they manufacture products which are expensive to transport in relation to their bulk, and that the vast majority of their product is absorbed by manufacturers in the metropolitan area. Their location pattern is strongly affected by these two factors.

About two-thirds of all the plants in these industries are concentrated in the urban clusters. Only 38 per cent of all the plants are to be found in the traditional urban core areas (39 per cent of all metal can plants, and 33 per cent of all glass container plants). These plants are often directly linked to manufacturers. For example, the M.J.B. Coffee Company has its own can producing plant, as does the California Packing Corporation. Similarly, Hunt Foods and Industries operates its own glass container plant. While the can producing industry is linked to all three major urban areas, the glass container industry is more strongly concentrated in the eastern part of the Bay Area. Of the fourteen plants in the sample, thirteen indicated that they served primarily a local market, and this market was totally composed of manufacturers.

The site requirements for both industries are quite high at 690,000 square feet and 491,460 square feet respectively. This, in turn, means that a central location, in terms of the industry's requirements, would not be economical. The majority of plants (90 per cent of the can manufacturers, and all of the glass container manufacturers) occupy a plant specifically built for them. Most plants are single storey (64 per cent) and all firms fully occupy their plant.

Important, in terms of location patterns, is that fact that thirteen of fourteen sample plants had railroad sidings. The requirement for railroad transportation is particularly marked with respect to the collection of non-local material inputs; eleven of thirteen plants indicated this was the primary method of collecting such inputs. For local inputs, and for both local and non-local market distribution, the truck is of major importance.

The nature of the product limits long distance transportation, because the product is bulky, of low-value, and readily liable to damage. Such considerations pull the industries close to their major sales outlets.

B. *LOCAL/REGIONAL MARKET INDUSTRIES*

There are four separate industries included in this general group; of the 76 sample plants forty serve a local market. The remaining thirty-six plants, however, on the basis of the *Census of Transportation* data for the respective industries, are considered to serve markets no larger than regional in size.

B.1. *Urban Core Oriented. Rail Transportation.* Industries S.I.C. 2851—Paints and Varnishes, and S.I.C. 3441—Fabricated Structural Steel (Figure 11).

These two industries are urban core oriented. Some 104 plants were identified in the Bay Area as of 1962, and 63 per cent of these were located in the urban cores centred on San Francisco and Oakland. They do not, however, seek C.B.D. locations, but are concentrated within the urban cores in the older industrial districts. Strengthening this type of location is that fact that elements within each industry have nuisance characteristics; in the fabrication of structural steel there is a large amount of noise, and in certain parts of the paint and varnish industry there is a fire hazard. They are industries, therefore, that would not be welcomed in a location adjacent, or close, to a residential area.

Of the thirty-eight sample plants included in this category, seventeen served a primarily local, and twenty-one a non-local, market.

Census of Transportation data indicates that an excess of 50 per cent of the products of these two industries are shipped within a range of 300 miles (Figure 12). The local market component is significant, therefore, but not dominant.

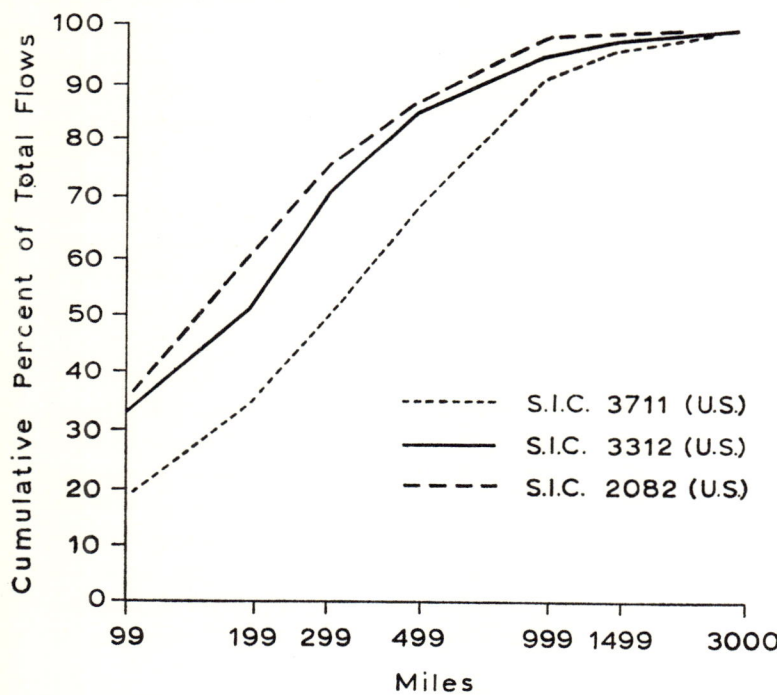

FIG. 17. MANUFACTURING FLOWS FOR THE ELECTRIC MEASURING INSTRUMENTS (S.I.C. 3611), ELECTRONIC COMPONENTS, N.E.C. (S.I.C. 3679), AND SEMICONDUCTORS (S.I.C. 3674)* INDUSTRIES BASED ON 1963 CENSUS OF TRANSPORTATION DATA.
*The 1958 Census included the Semiconductor Industry in S.I.C. 3679—Electronic Products, n.e.c.

The industry group is differentiated most markedly from the one that follows (B.2.) because of the need for railroad transportation; twenty-one of the thirty-eight plants possessed railroad sidings—a characteristic of the older industrial areas in any metropolis. The railroad was used largely as a means of collecting non-local material inputs, and for the distribution of the final product (the latter particularly so in the fabricated structural steel industry). Otherwise, truck was the major medium of transportation. Almost all local distribution, and input procurement, and a majority of distribution to non-local markets was through this medium.

The average site area for plants in this group is relatively low, but for the employee relatively high. This would seem to indicate, when taken together with the fact that the average plant size in both industries is relatively small, that these industries are well suited to the older industrial areas in which they are found. Location there means that their nuisance characteristics are relatively inconsequential to residential areas, and that their site requirements can be met.

In both industries there is a strong reliance on locally obtained inputs, indicating strong links with other industries in the area. These links are particularly apparent between the steel industry and steel fabricating, and beteween the chemical and petroleum refining industries and paints and varnishes.

B.2. *Urban Core Oriented. Truck Transportation.* Industries S.I.C. 2051—Bread and Related Products, and S.I.C. 2071—Candy (Figure 13).

This is a prime example of an industry group where the locational patterns are almost identical but where, using a strict local versus non-local market dichotomy, the two industries would not be placed in the same general location category. The bread and related products industry is strongly local market oriented (twenty of twenty-three sample plants had this characteristic) while the candy industry is strongly non-local (thirteen of fifteen sample plants). On the basis of *Census of Transportation* data, the candy industry at a national level has a median shipment distance in the 300–499 mile range. There is reason to suspect that because of San Francisco's location this distance may be less for the Bay Area industry.

This location type has about the same degree of concentration in the urban clusters and urban core areas (80 per cent and 66 per cent respectively) as does the preceding one. However, the site area per plant and per employee is small, and the industry type is strongly truck transportation oriented. Of the thirty-eight plants in the sample, only twelve possessed railroad sidings (31 per cent as compared with 55 per cent in the preceding B.1. category). Truck use was almost total in the case of distribution to the local

Intrametropolitan Manufacturing Location

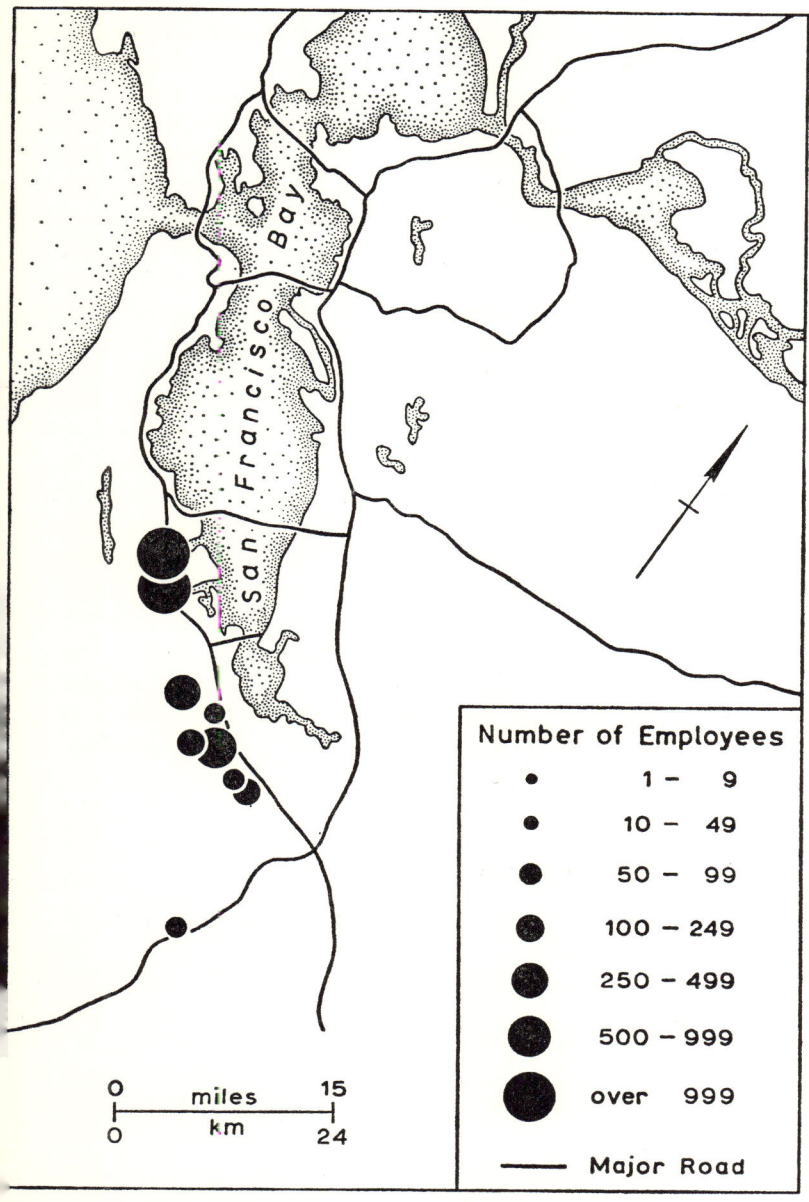

FIG. 18. LOCATION OF TUNGSTEN: ELECTRONIC TUBES PLANTS
(S.I.C. 3673)—SAN FRANCISCO BAY AREA, 1963.

and non-local markets, and in the acquisition of local inputs. In the case of non-local inputs this was less so; 48 per cent of all indicated inputs were transported by truck, 20 per cent by rail with freight forwarder, and only 20 per cent by rail. The latter figure compares with 38 per cent for the preceding (B.1.) group.

The products of this industry type are perishable to a degree, with baked goods being more so than candy. This means a need for rapid distribution. Some degree of concentration within the urban core is to be found; in each case this is in the older wholesaling districts. In Oakland and San Francisco, for example, some six of nine candy plants employing over 50 persons are located in the older wholesaling areas. The same is true of the larger baked products plants. Manufacturing of this type, together with 'wholesaling with stocks are classes of activity that require large amounts of space for the storage and handling of goods. They seek low-priced space generally found in the older buildings which tend to be concentrated in the older sections of the central district area.' (Mitchell and Rapkin, p. 116). This is confirmed by the large number of plants that occupy previously used space; of the thirty-eight sample plants, some twenty-one (55 per cent) occupy space of this nature. In addition, a substantial minority of firms have occupied their plant since before 1940 (39 per cent). As Pred has indicated, 'abandoned warehouses and multistory factory buildings are apparently particularly attractive to large scale food manufacturers.' (Pred, 1964a, p. 175).

C. *REGIONAL MARKET INDUSTRIES*

On the basis of questionnaire data obtained from the eleven sample plants in the three industries comprising this group, only three (of which two employ less than 100 persons) indicated that they served a local market. *Census of Transportation* data indicates that all three industries ship over, or close to in the case of the motor vehicle industry, 50 per cent of their products within a 300 mile range (Figure 14). These three industries can be divided into two distinct categories.

C.1. *Regional Market. Strong Urban Core Concentration.* Industry S.I.C. 2082—Malt Liquor (Figure 15).

Intrametropolitan Manufacturing Location

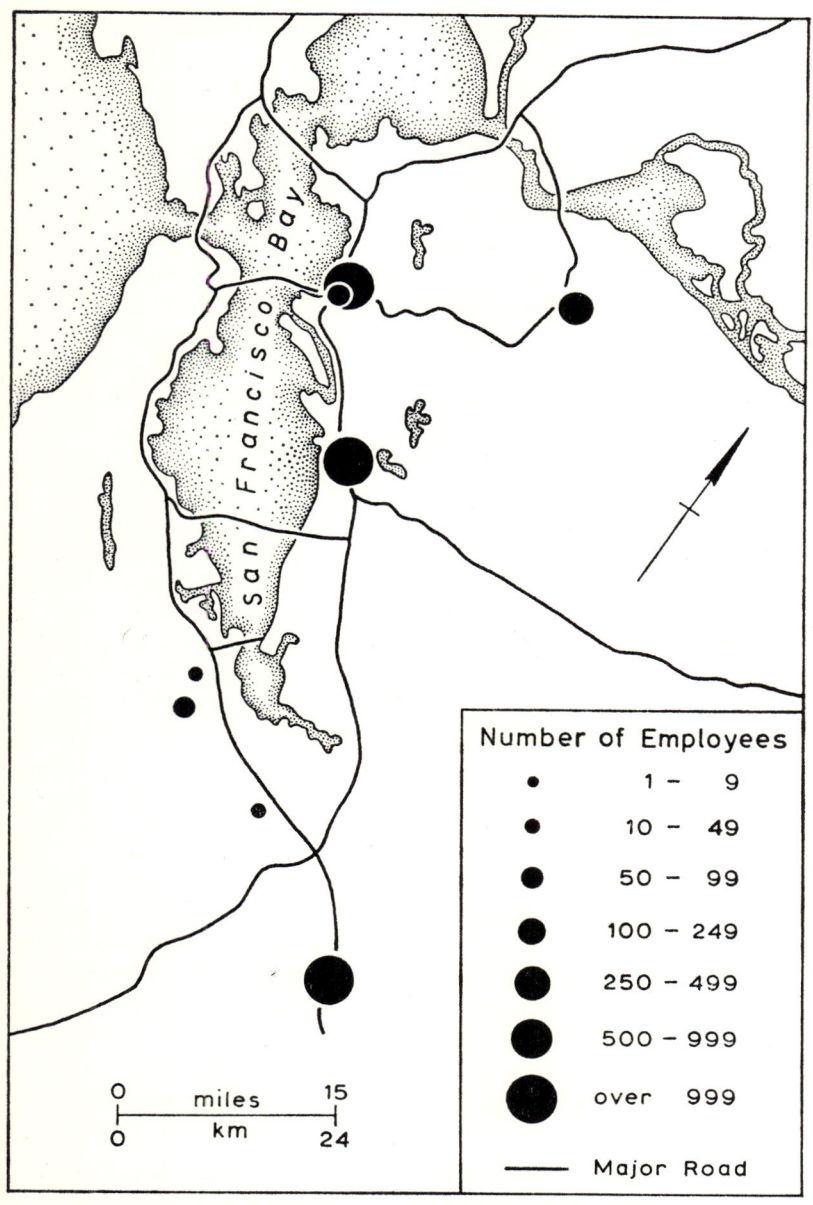

FIG. 19. LOCATION OF COMPUTING AND RELATED MACHINE PLANTS (S.I.C. 3571)—SAN FRANCISCO BAY AREA, 1963.

In the Bay Area this industry is strongly concentrated in San Franciso (four of five plants). Within that city there is an area of concentration; three plants are located around the intersection of the James Lick and Central Freeways, that is on the south-west periphery of the C.B.D. The single plant in San Jose is located on the north-west edge of the C.B.D. of that city.

The site area and per employee area requirements are above average, but the industry is one that is locationally static. The plant required is rather specialized and there is a history of the buying and selling of individual plants. Thus two major beer producers (Schlitz and Hamms) both occupy plants that were obtained from other brewing companies. This, combined with the early preference of beer plants for urban core locations, has meant the continuation of a location pattern probably set initially in the nineteenth century. All four plants sampled indicated multistory plants which were fully occupied.

The plants require a railroad siding, except when they are small. The three large plants in the sample all had railroad sidings that were used for the collection of inputs from local sources (66 per cent of cases), from non-local sources (80 per cent of cases), and to a highly limited degree for the distribution of the product outside the local market area. The railroad is a definite requirement and often, therefore, this industry is linked to the original railroad terminal area.

C.2. *Regional Market. Located Outside of Urban Core Areas.* Industries S.I.C. 3312—Blast Furnaces and Steel Mills (Figure 16), and S.I.C. 3711—Motor Vehicles.

The location pattern exemplified by these two industries is one of avoidance of the highly congested, high land value, urban core areas within the metropolis. There are ten plants in these two industries in the Bay Area; only three of these are in the urban clusters, and these are also within the urban core areas. The three plants in the urban core areas, however, are either small (one case), in a heavy industrial district (one case in Emeryville), or on the very periphery of the urban core area (one case in San Leandro). Also, of all ten plants only one is located on the west side of the Bay; the remainder are strung in a semicircle which extends from Milpitas (Santa Clara County) to Pittsburg (Contra Costa County).

The primary reasons for this location pattern are associated with the market area served and the site requirement of the plants. Both industries serve a regional market; six of eight sample plants stated that they served a non-local market, and *Census of Transportation* data indicate that for the blast furnace and steel mill industry the median distance of shipment (nationally) was between 100 and 199 miles, while for the motor vehicle industry it was between 300 and 499 miles. It has been indicated earlier that industries of this type are most numerous on that side of the metropolis facing the larger portion of the regional market. The evidence presented here would seem to support that contention, and is doubtless reinforced by the physical separation of the area under consideration.

Of primary interest is the large size of the average plant in these industries. For the United States in 1963, the average size of a blast furnace and steel mill industry plant was 1,780 employees, while for a motor vehicle plant it was 332. In addition, the space requirements for both industries are extremely high; both industries rank among the top five of the selected industries with respect to this criterion. The avoidance of urban core locations is reinforced in the case of the blast furnace and steel mill industry by certain nuisance characteristics; namely, noise, dirt, and continuous working.

Truck is the major transport medium to both local (86 per cent of cases) and non-local (63 per cent of cases) markets, and for the collection of local inputs. The railroad is of some importance in distributing to the non-local market (37 per cent of cases) but is of much greater importance in the collection of non-local inputs. In the latter case, rail accounted for about 50 per cent of the cases, the remainder being shared between rail with freight forwarder and truck. Of seven plants sampled, six had railroad sidings, the exception being the smallest of the motor vehicle plants.

D. *REGIONAL/MULTI-REGIONAL MARKET INDUSTRIES*

Forty-one sample plants were included in this category; of these only five (12 per cent) indicated that they served a local market. *Census of Transportation* data (see Figure 17) support the contention that the industries included in this category on the basis of their similar location patterns, have market areas which range from regional to multi-regional.

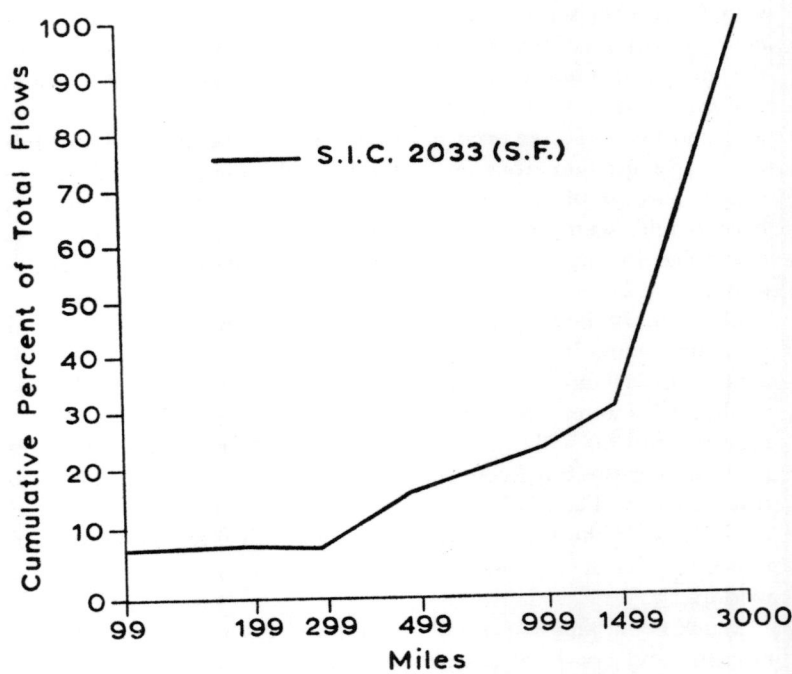

Fig. 20. Manufacturing Flows for the Canned Fruit and Vegetable (S.I.C. 2033) Industry based on 1963 Census of Transportation data.

D.1. *Concentrated 'Communication-Oriented' Industries Located Outside Urban Clusters.* Industries S.I.C. 3611—Electric Measuring Instruments, S.I.C. 3673—Tungsten: Electronic Tubes (Figure 18), and S.I.C. 3679—Electronic Products, n.e.c.

The three industries in this category were composed of seventy-two plants in the Bay Area in 1962. Of these, only 28 per cent were located in the urban clusters and only 15 per cent in the old urban core areas. However, some 54 per cent of the plants were located within eight miles of Palo Alto. There is then a strong concentration of plants away from any of the three central cities.

Site requirements both per plant and per employee are in the medium range. These requirements are inflated beyond the minimum because of the affinity of such electronic plants for landscaped, spacious sites. This is related to the type of personnel that the industries depend upon, the newness of the industries and the industrial park location of many of the plants. The sample data support these contentions; only six of the thirty-two sample firms were in previously occupied plants, and only one plant dated from prior to 1940.

The product is a high value one, particularly with respect to weight. In this location type, the presence of airline facilities close by is of some importance. Whereas in the local market area, both in terms of distribution of product and receipt of inputs, the truck is totally dominant, in the non-local market framework this is not the case. To the non-local market the most important transportation medium used is air freight (50 per cent of all cases), and for inputs obtained non-locally air is also of some importance (24 per cent of all cases). The balance of non-local inputs is truck transported. The high value of the product means that it can absorb heavy transportation charges, and it is often critical, of course, for the product to be delivered rapidly to the consumer whether he be the United States Government or a private manufacturer.

These industries are all of a scientific nature and realize 'external economies' through concentration. These economies are in terms of shared research facilities, the greater likelihood of maintaining the most up-to-date technology, the pool of scientific personnel which is available, and the presence of university research facilities (Stanford University). These are external economies which are not dependent on the clustering of the market as, for example, with letterpress printing.

D.2. *Randon Location Within Urban Clusters.* Industries S.I.C. 3511—Steam Engines, S.I.C. 3571—Computing and Related Machines (Figure 19), S.I.C. 1925—Guided Missiles, and S.I.C. 1931—Tanks and Tank Components.

The classification of this industry type is a good deal more tenuous than all others in this typology because of the nature of the industries (three separate industries were analysed as one

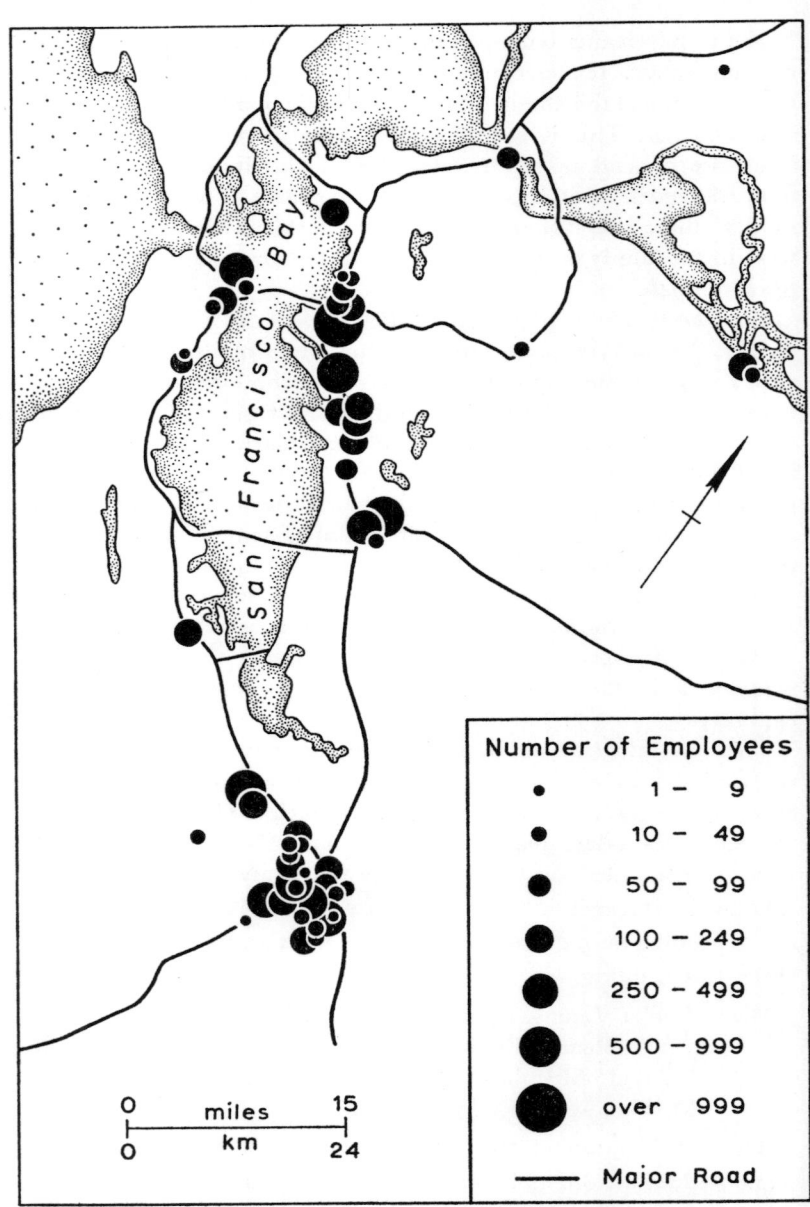

Fig. 21. Location of Canned Fruit and Vegetable Plants (S.I.C. 2033)—San Francisco Bay Area, 1963.

industry group because of disclosure problems) and the very limited size of the sample.

The locational pattern of these industries would appear to be due to a number of factors, few (if any) of which are related to those upon which the rest of this typology is built. While the four industries taken as a group display a preference for a location within an urban cluster (nine of the twelve plants occupy such a location), the attraction of an urban core location is minimal (only three of the twelve plants for this category). There is some attraction shown by the area between Palo Alto and San Jose, where half of the plants are to be found. All of the industries have certain factors in common.

First, they are all high value-added industries in which transportation costs are a minimal part of total production coats. Pred has pointed out that when 'an industry is essentially insensitive to transport considerations the locational attraction of particular rail, waterfront, and highway sites are minimized for most plants' (Pred, 1964a, p. 177), and, resultantly, location depends on a more fortuitous set of factors if there are no important agglomerative considerations.

Second, a majority of the plants in this group operate under Government contract and produce items for which there is no economic micro-location, but only (at a maximum) some regional location factors. Such industries as tank production and guided missile production are unlikely to be affected, in terms of location, by the usual set of economic factors. To this should be added that steam engine production is a highly 'customised' industry, often producing under Government contract, and resultantly has a wide range of locational choice within the metropolis.

Movement in the local market area (both of inputs and distribution of the final product) is entirely by truck transportation. Non-local movement varies according to the individual industry. The computing and related machinery industry uses truck (50 per cent of cases) and air (37 per cent of cases) for distribution of the final product. It should be pointed out that the bulk and weight of this industry's product, in comparison with the others in this group, is relatively small. The other three industries (S.I.C.'s 3511, 1931, and 1925) are more alike in their requirements. Distribution to the non-local market in these industries was largely by truck, with rail accounting for a minor share (33 per cent of cases) of the movement. In the collection of non-local inputs, the railroad played a more important role. Of twelve inputs obtained non-locally by all four industries, five were brought in by rail and seven by truck; rail was dominant in the tank industry (S.I.C. 1931) and in the computing and accounting machine industry (S.I.C. 3571).

All of the industries in this group have large site requirements per plant and per employee, and this, of course, forces a location away from the more densely urbanized and industrialized locations.

E. *MULTI-REGIONAL (NATIONAL) MARKET INDUSTRIES*

This includes one industry, canned fruit and vegetables, comprising fifty-five plants. In the sample of twenty-nine plants, all but two indicated they primarily served a non-local market. In addition, *Census of Transportation* data, based on the San Francisco production area, indicated that the median shipment distance for this industry was in excess of 1,500 miles (Figure 20). On this basis it was classified as a multi-regional (national) market industry.

E.1. *Concentrated Location Outside Urban Core Locations Local/ Regional Perishable Raw Materials.* Industry S.I.C. 2033— Canned Fruit and Vegetables (Figure 21).

The location pattern of this industry shows concentration in traditional areas inside the urban clusters (84 per cent of plants) but outside of the urban core areas (only 29 per cent of the plants are in such locations). The intermediate area of urban cluster minus urban core thus accounts for 55 per cent of all plants. The majority of plants are facing the areas of raw material supply. The greater Oakland area and the greater San Jose area account for all but thirteen of the plants. This is because the industry is tied to perishable raw material sources and it is necessary, therefore, for the distance between plant and raw materials to be minimized. There is also considerable inertia in the industry; nineteen of the twenty-seven sample plants are of pre-1940 vintage. In addition, the plants have remained in their present locations while the distance between them and their raw materials has increased; as, for example, with the San Jose cluster.

The site area required per plant and per employee is relatively high, which forces a location away from urban cores. Location is

Intrametropolitan Manufacturing Location

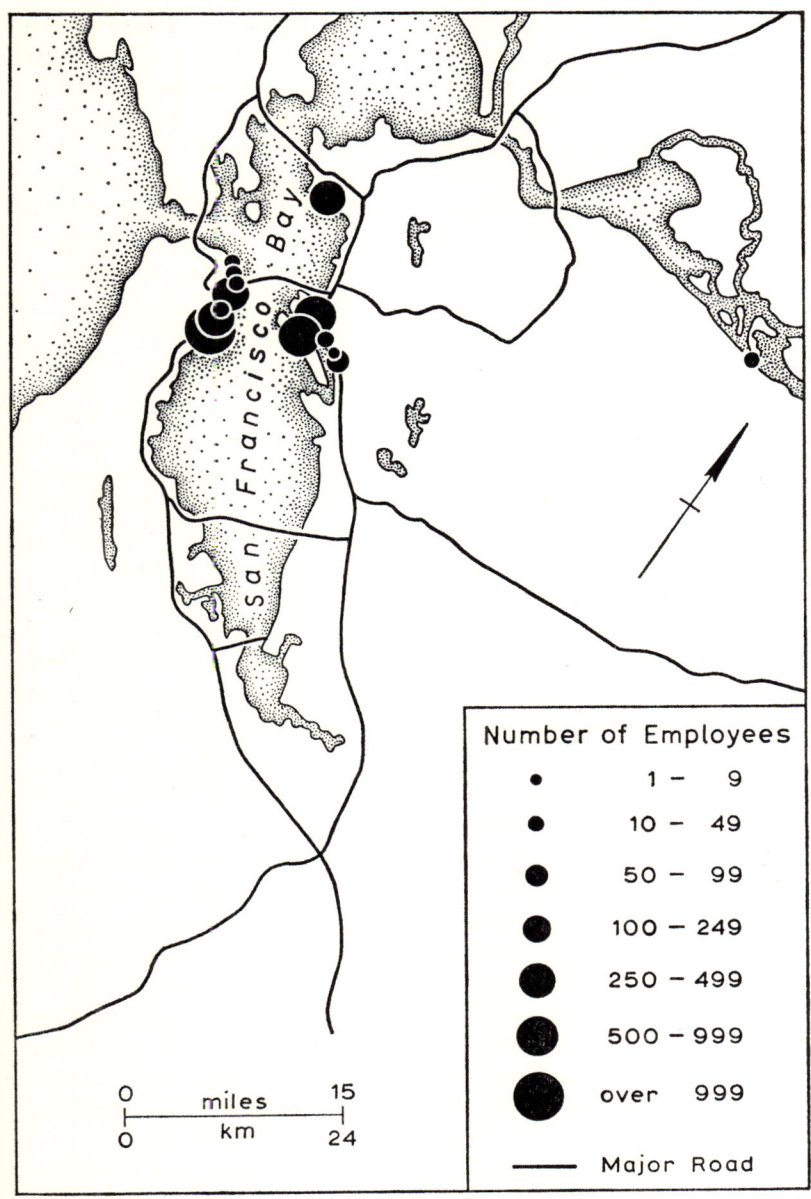

Fig. 22. Location of Shipbuilding and Repairing Plants (S.I.C. 3731)—San Francisco Bay Area, 1963.

also constrained by the need for railroad transportation; of the twenty-nine sample plants, twenty-six had a railroad siding. The railroad is used basically for delivery of the finished product to the national market; in all other material and product movements the truck is dominant. All plants are single story and a majority have been occupied previously. While the plants are raw material oriented, they are also labour oriented in that they need large summer labour supplies for the canning process. As a result, they cannot afford to be too far removed from major low-income residential concentrations.

F. WATERFRONT LOCATION

Two major distinctions are to be made between the two industries that fall into this category. One industry (petroleum refining) *prefers* a waterfront location, the other (shipbuilding) *requires* a waterfront location. Second, petroleum refining, because of the enormous site area required and, to a lesser extent, the fire hazard inherent in its product, seeks to find wide open areas close to the waterfront. On the other hand, shipbuilding with relatively smaller site requirements is often located on the industrial waterfront of the major cities. In the Bay Area, for example, only one very small specialized petroleum refining plant is located in an urban core area. Conversely, 86 per cent of the plants in the shipbuilding industry are in urban core locations.

F.1. *Waterfront: Urban Core Location.* Industry S.I.C. 3731—Shipbuilding and Repairing (Figure 22).

The site area requirements of this industry, although relatively high, are less than one-thirtieth of those for the petroleum refining industry. This, in itself, means a comparatively higher propensity for urban core location. Second, it is a service industry (to a degree) associated with port activity. Ship repairing takes place as close as possible to where the ship docks. The industry has maintained its late nineteenth century location pattern. The major concentrations are in the old ports of San Francisco and Oakland; of a total of fourteen plants, seven are in San Francisco and five in the Oakland-Alameda complex. The industry is also tied to local inputs.

As both the average size of plant and site area requirements are relatively high, the industry is located away from residential or

Intrametropolitan Manufacturing Location

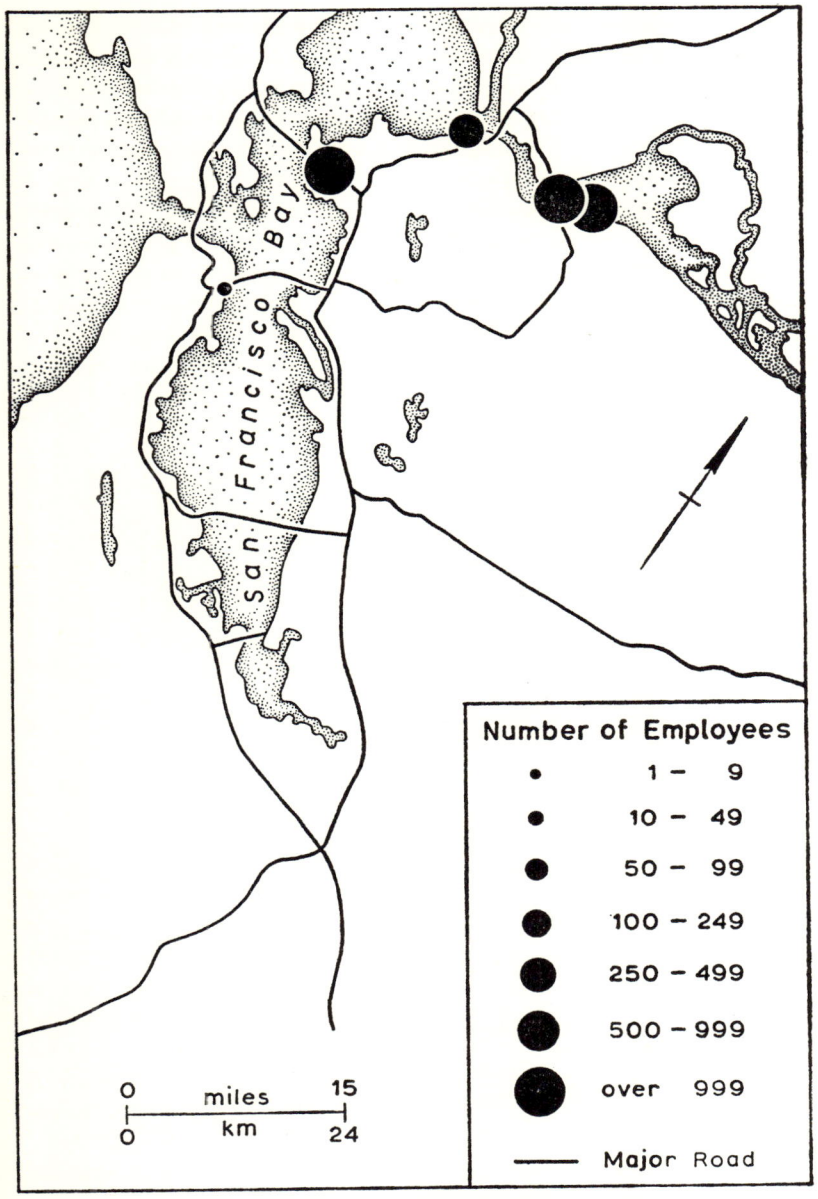

Fig. 23. Location of Petroleum Refining Plants (S.I.C.2911) —San Francisco Bay Area, 1963.

business land use. All plants, with one exception, had a railroad siding and the preferred location, therefore, is the belt of land that often lies between the railroad and the waterfront. The shipbuilding industry depends strongly on local inputs, most of which are transferred to the site by truck, but the railroad is important for the collection of non-local inputs.

It should be noted that not all occupiers of the waterfront use it in either a direct or indirect way. In Solzman's study of Chicago it was found that the use of the waterfront by manufacturing plants located on it, decreased towards the city centre (Solzman). Whatever the specific location, however, the degree of non-usage is high. In a study of the St. Louis region it was estimated that '35 per cent of the firms located on the river did not in fact use it directly in any way.' (Niland, p. 10). Solzman estimates the percentage of manufacturers located on the waterway in Chicago who presently make no use of their waterway at 42 per cent (Solzman, p. 50). Niland indicates that waterfront sites historically were good sites without regard to the inherent advantages of the waterfront itself, that the waterfront area 'because it includes some of the oldest section of the city, contains many structures which are now in the hands of a second or later generation of owners to whom the primary appeal has been simply that of inexpensive floor space.' (Niland, p. 11).

F.2. *Waterfront: Non-Urban Core Location.* Industry S.I.C. 2911— Petroleum Refining (Figure 23).

This industry is forced away from urban core areas because of its enormous site requirements and the fire hazard involved in its production process. The industry does not require a waterfront site if, for example, inputs are entirely piped to the refinery, but in any metropolitan area that has a waterfront petroleum refining is a prime candidate for such a location. The average plant size is large in terms of employment (1963 United States average—279 employees) and site area requirement. This industry, as with shipbuilding, usually possesses its own facilities for handling shipping in the form of a private bulkhead and wharf.

Crude oil inputs are shipped partially by barge and partially by pipeline; about 40 per cent by the former, and 60 per cent by the latter. Where pipeline is used together with barge, and where

TABLE 10
TYPOLOGY OF INTRAMETROPOLITAN MANUFACTURING LOCATIONS

Market Groupings	Industries in Study by S.I.C. Classification	
A. LOCAL MARKET INDUSTRIES		
1. C.B.D. Concentrated. Communication Oriented.	2751,	2752
2. Dispersed Location. Large Plants Urban Core Oriented. General Consumer Market.	2711,	2026
3. Bulky Product. Linked to Local Manufacturer.	3221,	3411
B. LOCAL/REGIONAL MARKET INDUSTRIES		
1. Urban Core Oriented. Rail Transportation.	2851	3441
2. Urban Core Oriented. Truck Transportation.	2051,	2071
C. REGIONAL MARKET INDUSTRIES		
1. Strong Urban Core Concentration.	2082	
2. Located Outside Urban Core Areas.	3312,	3711
D. REGIONAL/MULTI-REGIONAL MARKET INDUSTRIES		
1. Concentrated 'Communication-Oriented'. Located Outside Urban Clusters.	3611,	3673
2. Random Location Within Urban Clusters.	3511,	3571
	1925,	1931
E. MULTI-REGIONAL (NATIONAL) MARKET INDUSTRIES		
1. Concentrated Outside Urban Core Locations. Local/Regional Perishable Raw Materials.	2033	
F. WATERFRONT INDUSTRIES		
1. Urban Core Location.	3731	
2. Non-Urban Core Location.	2911	
G. ADDITIONS FROM LITERATURE*		
1. Local Market. Random Location, Some C.B.D. Association. Local Raw Material Sources.	2097	

*This location type is an addition from Pred, 1964a.

output is moved out largely by barge, the break of bulk point (in this case the waterfront) is the obvious location in that it minimizes terminal costs. Refined products are less homogeneous than crude oil; many are too viscous to be carried by pipeline. In the case of the Bay Area petroleum refining industry, outputs to the local market are moved largely by truck, and to the non-local market by barge (68 per cent of all cases). All five plants in the sample had railroad sidings, but these did not appear to be used for any major movement of inputs or outputs. All of the plants had been built specifically for the firms occupying them, and were of long standing; none of the five sample plants had begun operation since 1940.

The above twelve-fold typology accounts for all of the selected industries in this study. On the basis of previous work in the field of intrametropolitan analysis, however, it is deemed necessary in order to complete the typology to add what Pred has typed as 'Local Market Industries with Local Raw Material Sources.'

G.1. *Local Market Industries with Local Raw Material Sources.* Industry example S.I.C. 2097—Manufactured Ice.

This group includes industries whose raw materials are nearly ubiquitous, for example, those industries reliant on the by-products of local meat packing, iron and steel production, petroleum refining, etc. 'Industries in this category as a whole are often found in random locations because virtually all movement associated with product assembly and distribution occurs within the metropolis and thereby precludes orientation toward traditional railroad sites.' (Pred, 1964a, p. 176). Some degree of localization near the Central Business District is not uncommon.

Table 10 summarizes the thirteen types of intrametropolitan manufacturing locations.

CHAPTER 4

Conclusions

THE typology presented in the previous chapter is limited in its generality by the narrow basis of the research. Ideally, it should be founded on an analysis of the complete range of four-digit industries in a number of American metropolitan areas of recognizably different form. The research for this study was confined, however, to a single metropolitan area and to a limited number of industries, for which varying amounts of literature and data were available. Thus, one can only state that each of the types represents a group of industries having similar locational patterns within the San Francisco Bay Area. There are data that are not available that would improve this study; for example, information relating to plants leaving the metropolitan area (and the reasons for their action) would be useful in identifying areas of industrial decay. A typology of such areas would complement the locational typology resulting from this study.

'The conventional role of geographic analysis is to differentiate the earth's surface, to sort over and separate it into convenient areas of "like" characteristics.' (Haggett, p. 3). This, in fact, is the *raison d'être* for any typology with geographical foundations. In addition, of course, a typology or classification is the precondition to theory formulation (analytical models). In this case an attempt is being made to classify a series of locations into meaningful groupings using explicitly defined variables. Whilst each industry is, at one level, unique it is advantageous to assign them to broad classes of locations. The gains that come from this classification process may or may not outweigh the losses in accuracy: 'science is always trying to invent new, more efficient categories in a neverending attempt to pigeon-hole reality in more and more accurate terms.' (Haggett, p. 3). At the same time there is, by inference, an identification (however incomplete) of the forces which have operated to produce the specific location patterns. The typology, therefore, represents the patterns produced as the end result of a series of dynamic evolutions. These incorporate, for example changing transportation technology and external economies, and reflect the 'tremendous inertia of forms, functions, and locations.' (Pred, 1964a, p. 180).

The typology also represents an advance over two general themes which run through the industrial location literature. The first revolves around the classification of industrial locations based on tenuous distinctions. Many writers classify industry as being either 'heavy' or 'light', 'local market' or 'non-local market', 'processing' or 'fabricating'. None of these distinctions taken alone is particularly helpful in the rigorous identification of locational types. The second theme is the use of the concept of industrial zones or areas; that is, the use of industry as a homogeneous land-use definition (Stefaniak, 1963; Loewenstein, 1963). Some comment is usually introduced in this approach as to the types of industry that would locate in each industrial zone. Sometimes this is highly simplified as in the case of Harris and Ullman's differentiation between 'heavy', 'light' and 'industrial suburb' manufacturing (Harris and Ullman, p. 10). At other times, it is more elaborate in that a 'model of the spatial industrial structure of a metropolis' (Hamilton) is produced. In neither case is this more than the identification of industrial land-use patterns in a metropolitan area, with or without some reference to the industries located in each discrete zone. This, in turn, leads to the repetitious use of particular industries as exemplifying particular location types. Hamilton, for example, states that 'central locations are occupied by industries in which the need for the best access to skilled labour from the whole area (e.g. instruments, tools, printing), to the central business district (e.g. clothing, office machinery), and to the whole urban market for distribution (e.g. services, newspapers) offsets high land costs.' (Hamilton, pp. 408–9). As a result of this type of analysis, large numbers of industries (the majority in fact) are excluded from consideration in any industrial location classification. This study has taken the opposite approach. A range of industries was studied in detail, and an attempt then made to generalize the resulting location patterns. In this sense, the produced typology is much more inclusive.

The results of this study are directly helpful in assessing the realistic applicability of the descriptive and empirical studies outlined earlier. The 'concentric zone' theory of Burgess is lamentably weak in dealing with manufacturing. It allows for only one zone of wholesaling and light manufacturing adjacent to the Central Business District. It, therefore, takes no account of the variety of location types lying away from the central city, and assumes that all manufacturing is of the 'light' variety. The 'sector theory' of Hoyt suffers from the allocation of all industry to a single light manufacturing class concentrated in an axial belt. The 'multiple nuclei' theory of Harris and Ullman distinguishes three industrial districts within the metropolitan area: 'light' manufacturing, 'heavy' manufacturing, and 'industrial suburb.' This again perpetuates the notion that it is possible to meaningfully separate 'heavy' from 'light' industry and that they are spatially segregated. No generally acceptable formula for distinguishing 'light' from 'heavy' industry exists, and even assuming this distinction as a realistic possibility, it is apparent that the two types of industry are intermixed in industrial land-use areas. Isard's 'optimal urban land use pattern' contains some ideas that are borne out by this study. All producers of a given commodity are concentrated in the same industrial district excepting those firms 'which manufacture miscellaneous items or use ubiquitous raw materials.' (Isard, p. 278). It must be admitted that no industrial location type in this study has these specific characteristics. This approach of Isard does, however, produce a valuable dichotomy between the high concentration of some industries and the high dispersion of the remainder. In general, the typology supports this contention; in reality there is a broad range of location types which range between these two extremes.

Isard, in addition, recognizes that his optimal pattern can be disturbed by a variety of factors. 'Technology, physical and cultural environment, legal institutions, and other factors serve to impose restraints as well as distortions upon otherwise rational land-use patterns.' (Isard, p. 280).

Haig's notions, particularly in terms of the characteristics of industries that cling to central city locations, have held up well under further analysis. His study, however, did not produce a typology but rather a set of characteristics for industries at two ends of a spectrum: those industries clinging to a central site and those avoiding such a location. As such, for the purposes of this analysis, it has the same pitfalls as the work of Isard. A critical feature of the typology is that it admits to the possibility of a series of industrial location types. Any concept that revolves around dichotomies is, therefore, inadequate.

Comment should also be made on the fact that in the case of the *smaller* plants in those industries having an intimate adjustment to the local consumer market (for example, the fluid milk and newspaper industries), there is a relationship between the location pattern of such industries and the spatial equilibrium model of Lösch. In the Löschian framework, market oriented activities do not cluster, as do the large plants in the newspaper industry, because each unit has a spatial monopoly. Also, of course, in Löschian analysis all industries are market oriented which is a very limited aspect of the model. This form of analysis has been used in the study of the commercial structure of the San Francisco Bay Area (Vance, 1962). There appears to be some possibility of extending this form of analysis to certain of the local market, consumer oriented, industries.

This study overcomes the ambiguities inherent in the contributions outlined above by formulating a more realistic, empirically derived, framework for the analysis of industrial location within the metropolitan context. It also poses a number of questions, apart from those already indicated, which require further investigation. The typology is based on the study of a single, unique, metropolitan area and should at this stage, therefore, be considered speculative. While the typology has a strong spatial component, the time component has been given a subordinate role, except insofar as past location decisions have affected contemporary location patterns. Would a similar typology produced for certain critical times in the industrial history of the San Francisco Bay Area throw additional light upon the changing locational requirements of specific industries and/or specific locational types? With such a series of typologies it might then be possible to produce a tentative growth model (with spatial dimensions) for intrametropolitan industrial location. This would be an alternative to, but also complement directly, other approaches to the same problem; diffusion studies, urban simulation models, changing spatial profitability margins over time for specific industries in cities, etc.

The problem of identifying linkages between industries is, of course, a long continuing one. Linkages, in the spatial rather than the economic sense, have largely been deduced by spatial association. This is a research problem in which this form of study could make some contribution if it could be extended to a wider range of metropolitan areas. Input-output studies give some clues to spatial linkages, but these are limited in view of the fact that the input-output technique is largely for a spatial economic analysis. Limitations are also introduced by the inverse relationship between the degree of disaggregation of industry and the size of the spatial unit of study; that is, the greatest degree of disaggregation is found at the national level. The concept of spatial linkages is firmly tied to that of 'external economies'. 'These are the advantages or disadvantages that arise from the close proximity of the plant to other activities.' (Alonso, 1964b, p. 104). External economies, or diseconomies, are extremely difficult to quantify. One approach to this problem would be to measure the spatial association of plants at a disaggregated level.

In conclusion, it should be stated that the need for detailed studies at the metropolitan level in industrial geography is evident. There is a reciprocal relationship between empirical studies and the production of more satisfying intra-urban theories. 'Industrial geography is concerned with the description and interpretation of the real world rather than with the derivation of abstract theory. Consequently, the student of industrial location has to go to the work of economists . . . for a thorough grounding in location theory. But much of this work is aimed at bringing the space dimension into conventional economic theory rather than providing a background from which to embark on empirical studies of industrial geography.' (Smith, D. M., p. 95). The opposite can be contended, namely that relevant theory must await upon adequate empirical information. Identification of significant variables at the metropolitan level through empirical research is necessary before significant new theoretical and/or conceptual contributions can be made.

The typology should be recognized as tentative, with recognition made of the limitations of the research. The amount of research concerned with metropolitan manufacturing location, which meets the minimal requirements for such a study, is small. This study provides some preliminary research conclusions which, if a viable and generally acceptable typology is to be produced, should be subjected to further testing.

REFERENCES

ALDERSON ASSOCIATES, INC., 1958. *Studies of Selected Industrial Groups for Factors Affecting Plant Location Decisions with Reference to the Industrial Environments of Philadelphia*, (Philadelphia).

ALONSO, W., 1964. (a) *Location and Land Use*, (Cambridge, Mass.).

ALONSO, W., 1964. (b) 'Location Theory', in *Regional Development and Planning: A Reader*, ed. by J. Friedmann and W. Alonso, (Cambridge, Mass.).

BANCROFT, H. H., 1890. *History of California*, (San Francisco), Vol. VII.

BARTHOLOMEW, H., 1965. *Land Uses in American Cities*, (Cambridge, Mass.).

BURGESS, E. W., 1925. 'The Growth of the City', *The City*, eds. R. E. Park, E. W. Burgess and R. D. McKenzie, (Chicago).

CALIFORNIA STATE RECONSTRUCTION AND RE-EMPLOYMENT COMMISSION, 1944. *Bay Region Takes Stock* (San Francisco).

CHINITZ, B., 1960. *Freight and the Metropolis* (Cambridge, Mass.).

DE MEIRLIER, M. J., 1950. *Manufactural Occupance in the West Central Area of Chicago*, (Chicago).

DICKENS, A. E., 1939. *The Growth and Structure of Real Property Uses in Indianapolis*, (Bloomington).

DUNCAN, O. D. et al., 1960. *Metropolis and Region*, (Baltimore).

ESTALL, R. C. and MARTIN, J. E., 1957-58. 'Industry in Greater London', *Town Planning Review*, 28, 261-277.

FLORENCE, P. S., 1948. *Investment, Location and Size of Plant* (Cambridge).

GARRISON, W. L. et al., 1959. *Studies of Highway Development and Geographic Change* (Seattle, Wash.).

GONEN, A., 1968. 'Intra-Urban Location of Manufacturing: The Case of Tel Aviv—Yafo', Paper presented to the XXIst International Geographical Congress, New Delhi, India.

GRAS, N. S. B., 1922. *An Introduction to Economic History*, (New York).

GRIFFIN, J. I., 1956. *Industrial Location in the New York Area*, (New York).

HAGGETT, P., 1965. *Location Analysis in Human Geography*, (London).

HAIG, R. M., 1927. *Major Economic Factors in Metropolitan Growth and Arrangement*, (New York).

HALL, P., 1962. *The Industries of London Since 1861*, (London).

HAMILTON, I., 1967. 'Models of Industrial Location', in *Models in Geography* ed. by R. J. Chorley and P. Haggett, (London).

HARRIS, C. D., and ULLMAN, E. L., 1945. 'The Nature of Cities', *Annals of the American Academy of Political and Social Science*, 242, 7-17.

HARVEY, R. O., 1951. *Land Uses in Bloomington, Indiana, 1818–1950*, (Bloomington).

HINKEL, E. J. and MCCANN (eds.), 1939. *Oakland 1852–1938*, (Oakland).

HOOVER, E., 1948. *The Location of Economic Activity*, (New York).

HOOVER, E. and VERNON, R., 1959. *Anatomy of a Metropolis*, (Cambridge, Mass.).

HOYT, H., 1939. *The Structure and Growth of Residential Neighborhoods in American Cities*, (Washington D.C.).

HURD, R. M., 1903. *Principles of City Land Values*, (New York).

ISARD, W., 1956. *Location and the Space Economy*, (New York).

JANASSON, O., 1957. *Industriutyeckling och Industrilokalisering i Göteborg* (Göteborg).

JONES, B. G., 1960. 'The Theory of the Urban Economy', Unpublished Ph.D. dissertation, University of North Carolina.

KENYON, J. B., 1960. *Industrial Localization and Metropolitan Growth: The Patterson-Passaic District*, (Chicago).

KERR, D. and SPELT, J., 1957. 'Manufacturing in Downtown Toronto', *Geographical Bulletin*, 10, 5–22.

LAMPARD, E. E., 1955. 'The History of Cities in the Economically Advanced Areas', *Economic Development and Cultural Change*, 3, 81–136.

LICHTENBERG, R., 1960. *One Tenth of a Nation*, (Cambridge, Mass.).

LINGE, G. J., 1963. 'The Diffusion of Manufacturing in Auckland, New Zealand', *Economic Geography*, 39, 23–39.

LOEWENSTEIN, L. K., 1965. *The Location of Residences and Work Places in Urban Areas*, (New York).

LOEWENSTEIN, L. K., 1963. 'The Location of Urban Land Uses', *Land Economics*, 39, 407–420.

LOGAN, M. I., 1964. (a) 'Manufacturing Decentralization in the Sydney Metropolitan Area', *Economic Geography*, 40, 151–162.

LOGAN, M. I., 1964. (b) 'Suburban Manufacturing: A Case Study', *Australian Geographer*, 9, 223–234.

LOWER MAINLAND REGIONAL PLANNING BOARD OF BRITISH COLUMBIA, 1960. *Manufacturing Industries in the Lower Mainland of British Columbia*, (Vancouver).

LOWRY, I. S., 1963. *Portrait of a Region*, (Pittsburgh).

MARR, P. D., 1955. 'Industrial Geography of the San Francisco North Bay'. Unpublished M.A. thesis, University of California, Berkeley.

MARTIN, J. E., 1966. *Greater London. An Industrial Geography*, (London).

MAYER, H. M., 1942. 'Patterns and Recent Trends of Chicago's Outlying Business Centers', *Journal of Land and Public Utility Economics*, 18, 4–16.

McKENZIE, R. D., 1933. *The Metropolitan Community*, (New York).

MINING AND SCIENTIFIC PRESS (April 5, 1902).

MITCHELL, W. N., 1933. *Trends in Industrial Location in the Chicago Region*, (Chicago).

MITCHELL, R. B. and RAPKIN, C., 1954. *Urban Traffic. A Function of Land Use* (New York).

NIKLASON, C. R., 1930. *Commercial Survey of the Pacific Southwest*, (Washington D.C.).

NILAND, P., 1961. *The Role of River Sites in the Industrial Development of the St. Louis Region*, (St. Louis).

PEGRUM, D. F., 1963. *Urban Transport and the Location of Industry in Metropolitan Los Angeles*, (Los Angeles).

PRED, A. R., 1966 *The Spatial Dynamics of U.S. Urban-Industrial Growth, 1800–1914* (Cambridge, Mass).

PRED, A. R., 1964 (a) 'The Intrametropolitan Location of American Manufacturing', *Annals of the Association of American Geographers*, 54, 165–180.

PRED. A. R., 1964. (b) 'Toward a Typology of Manufacturing Flows', *Geographical Review*, 54, 65-84.

RATCLIFF, R. U., 1949. *Urban Land Economics*, (New York).

RATCLIFF, R. U., 1955. 'The Dynamics of Efficiency in the Locational Distribution of Urban Activities', *The Metropolis in Modern Life*, ed. R. M. Fisher, (New York).

RODGERS, A., 1960. *The Industrial Geography of the Port of Genoa*, (Chicago).

SMITH, D. M., 1966. 'A Theoretical Framework for Geographical Studies of Industrial Location', *Economic Geography*, 42, 95-113.

SMITH, W., 1942. *The Distribution of Population and the Location of Industry on Merseyside*, (Liverpool).

SOLZMAN, D., 1966. *Waterway Industrial Sites: A Chicago Case Study*, (Chicago).

STANDARD INDUSTRIAL CLASSIFICATION MANUAL, 1957, (Washington D.C.).

STEDMAN, F., 1962. 'The California Peninsula: Laboratory of the New Industrial Age', *Industrial Development and Manufacturers Record*, 131, 34–48.

STEFANIAK, N. J., 1962. *Industrial Location Within the Urban Area*. (Madison).

STEFANIAK, N. J., 1963. 'A Refinement of Haig's Theory', *Land Economics*, 40, 428–433.

STEVENS, B. H., BRACKETT, C. A. and COUGHLIN, R. E., 1966. *An Investigation of Location Factors Influencing the Economy of the Philadelphia Region*, (Philadelphia).

THOMAS, L. F., 1927. *The Localization of Business Activities in Metropolitan St. Louis*, (St. Louis).

THOMPSON, W. R., 1965. *A Preface to Urban Economics*, (Baltimore).

TUNNARD, C. and REED, H. H., 1955. *American Skyline*, (Boston).

ULLMAN, E. L., 1962. 'The Nature of Cities Reconsidered', *Paper and Proceedings of the Regional Science Association*, 9, 7–23.

U.S. BUREAU OF THE CENSUS, 1966. *1963 Census of Transportation, Commodity Transportation Survey*, (Washington D.C.).

VANCE, J. E., 1960. 'Labor-Shed, Employment Field, and Dynamic Analysis in Urban Geography', *Economic Geography*, 36, 189-220.

VANCE, J. E., 1962. 'Emerging Patterns of Commercial Structure in American Cities', in *The I.G.U. Symposium in Urban Geography Lund 1960*, (Lund), 485–518.

VANCE, J. E., 1964. *Geography and Evolution in the San Francisco Bay Area* (Berkeley).

WEBER, A., 1929. *Theory of the Location of Industries*, (Chicago).

WEDERVANG, F., 1965. *Development of a Population of Industrial Firms* (Bergen).

WEISS, D. L., 1962. 'The Rail Network as an Element in the Growth of Population in the San Francisco Suburbs'. Unpublished M.A. thesis, University of California, Berkeley.

WENDT, P. F., 1957. 'Theory of Urban Land Values', *Land Economics*, 33, 228–240.

WILLIAM-OLSSON, W., 1940. 'Stockholm: Its Structure and Development', *Geographical Review*, 30, 430–433.

WINGO, L., 1961. *Transportation and Urban Land*, (Washington D.C.).

Soc
HC
108
S7
G76